NOVA SCO[...] PICTORIAL

Country Inns

Bed & Breakfast and much more

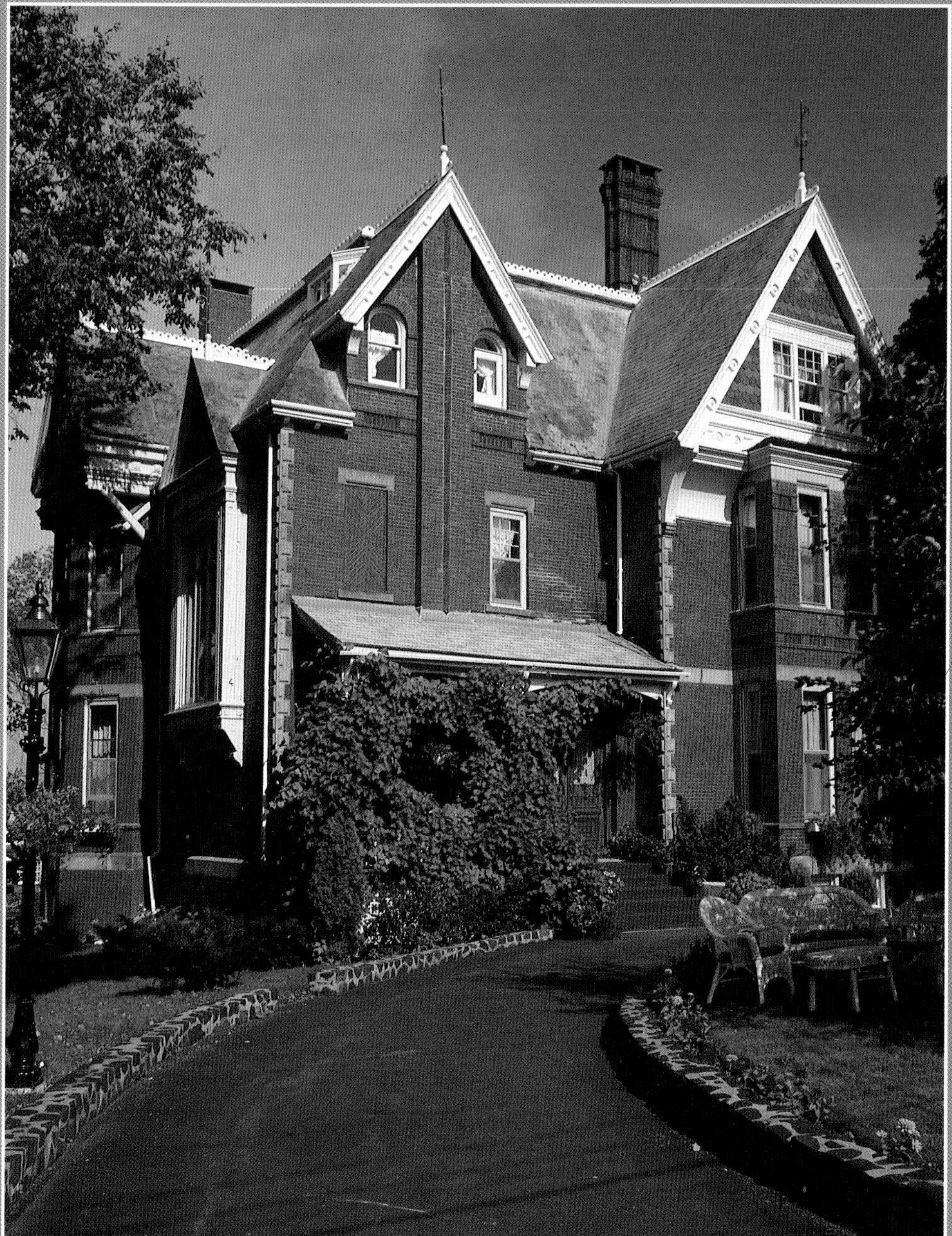

JAMES-STONEHOUSE PUBLICATIONS LIMITED

Cover
Tattingstone Inn, Wolfville

Title Page
Bread & Roses, Annapolis Royal

Introduction Page
White Point Beach Lodge,
White Point Beach

Below
Poplar Grove, Hants County

James-StoneHouse Publications Ltd.
PO Box 428
Dartmouth, Nova Scotia
Canada B2Y 3Y5

Canadian Cataloguing in Publication Data
Hines, Sherman, 1941-
Nova Scotia pictorial country inns, bed & breakfast, and much more.

ISBN 0-921128-31-2

1. Bed and breakfast accommodations - Nova Scotia - Pictorial works. 2. Bed and breakfast accommodations - Nova Scotia - Directories. 3. Hotels, taverns, etc. - Nova Scotia - Pictorial works. 4. Hotels, taverns, etc. - Nova Scotia - Directories. 5. Nova Scotia - Description and travel - 1981 - Views. I. Title.

TX910.C2H55 647.94716'03
C90-090998-6

The Publisher wishes to express its sincere gratitude to Tourism Nova Scotia for its maps, route logos, photographs, and other kind assistance and advice.

Apart from the Nova Scotia Accommodations Grading information, all other details contained in this book were supplied by the individual businesses and institutions. The Publisher has made every effort to ensure that the information is up-to-date but wishes to state that neither James-StoneHouse Publications Ltd. nor Tourism Nova Scotia is in any way responsible for this material. Inclusion in the book also does not constitute an endorsement of any establishment.

Printed for James-StoneHouse Publications Ltd. in Hong Kong

Project Manager: Deborah Field
Text and Editing: Paddy Muir
Graphic Design: GDA Inc.
Typesetting: GDA Inc.
Sales and Marketing: Susan Helpard
General Manager: J. Daniel Sargeant
Photo Credits: see page 182

Nova Scotia Accommodations Grading Program

The Tourism Industry Association of Nova Scotia, along with its counterpart in Prince Edward Island, has established a set of standards for various types of roofed accommodations. (New Brunswick joins in 1991, Newfoundland later.) Properties voluntarily participate in the program and pay an annual fee to be graded. Many of the accommodations in this edition of Nova Scotia Country Inns carry this grading which you'll find coded as follows:

Grade Star Descriptions

★	*Basic, clean, comfortable accommodation*
★★	*Basic, clean, comfortable accommodation with some amenities*
★★★	*Better quality accommodation; greater range of facilities and services*
★★★★	*High quality accommodation; extended range of facilities, amenities and guest services*
★★★★★	*Deluxe accommodation; the greatest range of facilities, amenities and guest services*

ATLANTIC CANADA ACCOMMODATIONS

RECOMMENDED

Trust in our stars!
★★★★★

Categories*

Hotels/Motels (H/M): *Large hotels, small hotels, motels, motor hotels*

Inns (I/B&B): *Country inns, bed & breakfasts, farm vacation homes, tourist homes*

Resorts (R): *Resorts having recreation facilities*

Sport Lodge/Cottages (SL/C): *Fishing and hunting lodges, cottages and cabins*

(*Note: Some properties have a mix of types of accommodation. In these cases an average star grade has been awarded.)

- ● Bed & Breakfast
- ▲ Inn
- ♦ Museum/Attraction
- ■ Shop/Gallery
- ✖ Restaurant/Lounge
- ▮ Resort
- ★ Atlantic Canada Accommodations Grading Program

People come to Nova Scotia for all sorts of reasons. They come to watch whales and birds, to hike the trails, fish and canoe the waterways. They come for the dozens of local festivals and celebrations for which our summers are famous. Many come just for the peace and quiet — a chance to get away from the hurly-burly of home and have someone else take care of the housekeeping and the meals for a while.

Whatever your reasons, you'll be well-received here. In fact, half the pleasure of a visit to Nova Scotia is getting to know Nova Scotians — and there's no better way than by staying with us. Throughout the province you'll find beautifully restored farm, country and town houses — and some brand-new ones too — with doors wide open to welcome travellers. Inns, bed and breakfasts, resort hotels, each (as you'll see when you browse through the pages of this book) offering something unique. What they have in common is Nova Scotia's renowned hospitality. Sleep under a different roof each night or choose a single base

When planning a visit be sure to give yourself plenty of time for exploring Nova Scotia's backroads. Cresting a small, blind hill you'll discover a hidden valley of white farmhouses, red barns and cattle-spotted hillsides, looking just like a child's toy farm. In one small town many homes perch on stilts; in another the tall, shingled houses bordering the steep streets sport widows' walks and ginger- bread trim. An unexpected stream tumbles down a rock face and runs beside the road to a perfect picnic spot beneath willows. Open the front door of an historic house, perfectly restored as a museum, and step back 200 years or more in time.

If your visit includes some time in the province's capital you'll find history co-existing peacefully side by side with the 1990s there. In the Halifax-Dartmouth area you can explore a fort or an old church, take a bus or walking tour, view the harbour by boat, visit an art gallery, shop and then finish your day with an elegant dinner and entertainment.

from which to explore, the choice is yours and the pleasure of your company is ours.

During your excursions, do drop in at the local craft shops and galleries along the way and discover examples of Nova Scotian artisans' fine work. Choose an unusual accent for your own home or a gift to take back for someone special, or just browse — and don't be afraid to ask how things are made or about their history. You'll find the craftspeople and gallery staff have lots of interesting information to share.

Surrounded by sea, you'd expect Nova Scotians to be experts when it comes to seafood. We are! Whether your preference is humble chowder or elegant salmon, lobster with all the trimmings or a plate of steaming mussels — restaurants, dining rooms and teahouses around the province offer tempting dishes to suit every taste. Choose seafood by all means — but don't forget to check the dessert menu too!

And of course there's always the sea. Winding over towering cliffs, the Cabot Trail plunges for frequent close-ups of wave-lapped beaches. The same sea slides silently into the salt marshes by Risser's Beach with its nesting seabirds. It rises and falls in 50-foot tides on the shores of the Bay of Fundy, leaving brightly painted fishing boats high and dry at their moorings. Waves to delight the surfer hurl themselves on Lawrencetown Beach, while a few miles away the sea's surface lies still and opalescent under an early-morning fog bank floating beyond deserted white sands.

Energetic hikes or gentle rambles; the silent meditation of a trout stream or the excitement of a festival, Nova Scotia has something to fit your mood — every day of your stay. We hope this book will help you plan your own perfect visit and keep its memories alive long after. Just remember — here in Nova Scotia we love having company come to stay!

Halifax Dartmouth

Lighthouse Route

Evangeline Trail

Glooscap Trail

Sunrise Trail

Cape Breton Trails

Marine Drive

*Note: an alphabetical index of establishments
is found on page 180

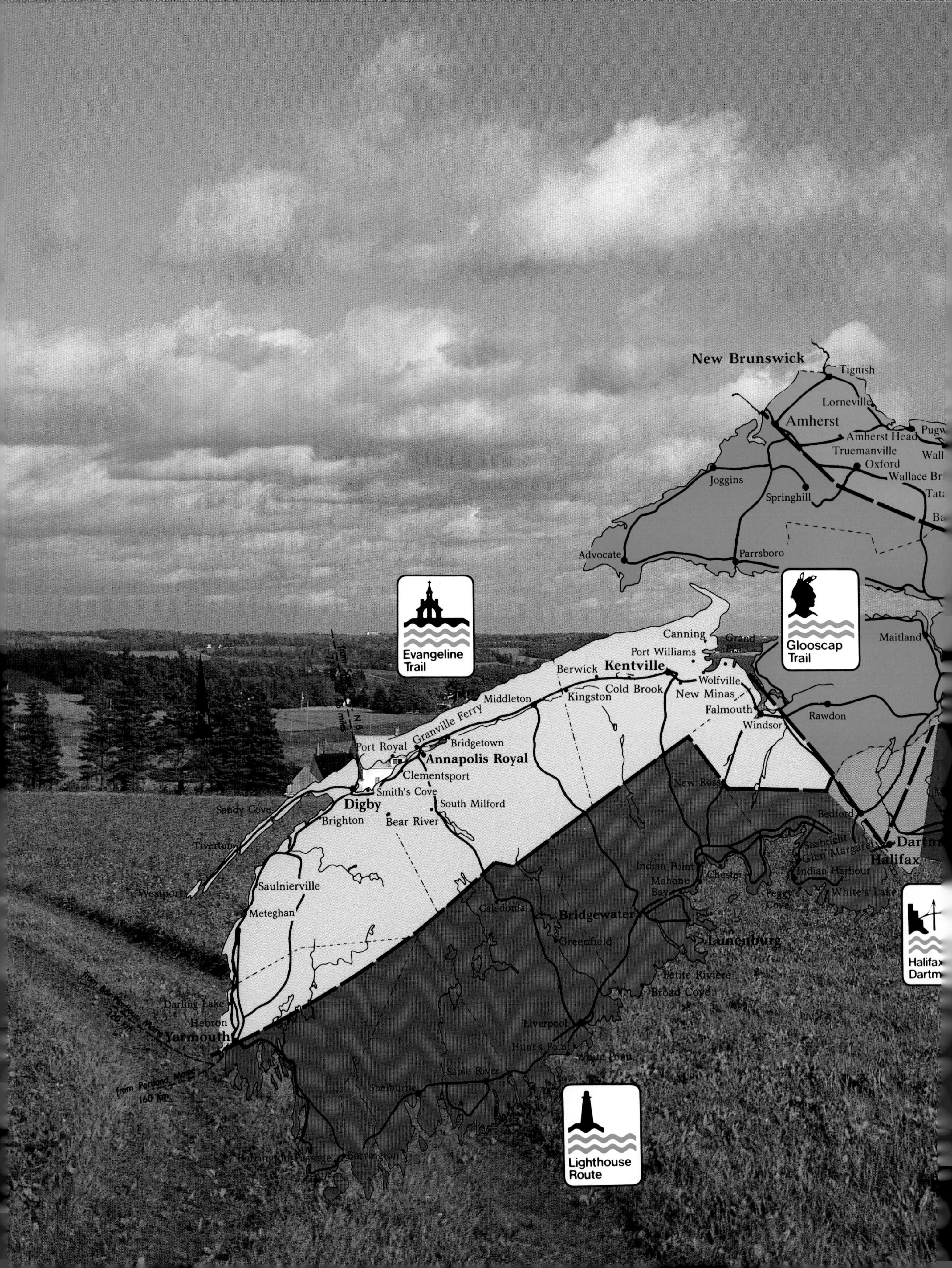
New Brunswick
Tignish
Lorneville
Amherst
Amherst Head
Truemanville
Oxford
Joggins
Springhill
Advocate
Parrsboro
Evangeline Trail
Glooscap Trail
Canning
Grand Pré
Port Williams
Berwick
Kentville
Wolfville
Cold Brook
Kingston
New Minas
Middleton
Falmouth
Windsor
Rawdon
Maitland
Granville Ferry
Port Royal
Bridgetown
Annapolis Royal
Clementsport
Smith's Cove
Digby
Sandy Cove
Brighton
Bear River
South Milford
New Ross
Bedford
Tiverton
Westport
Saulnierville
Meteghan
Seabright
Glen Margaret
Halifax
Indian Harbour
Indian Point
Chester
Mahone Bay
Peggy's Cove
White's Lake
Caledonia
Bridgewater
Lunenburg
Greenfield
Petite Rivière
Broad Cove
Darling Lake
Hebron
Yarmouth
Liverpool
Hunt's Point
White Point
Sable River
Shelburne
from Portland, Maine 160 Km
Barrington
Barrington Passage
Lighthouse Route
Halifax Dartm

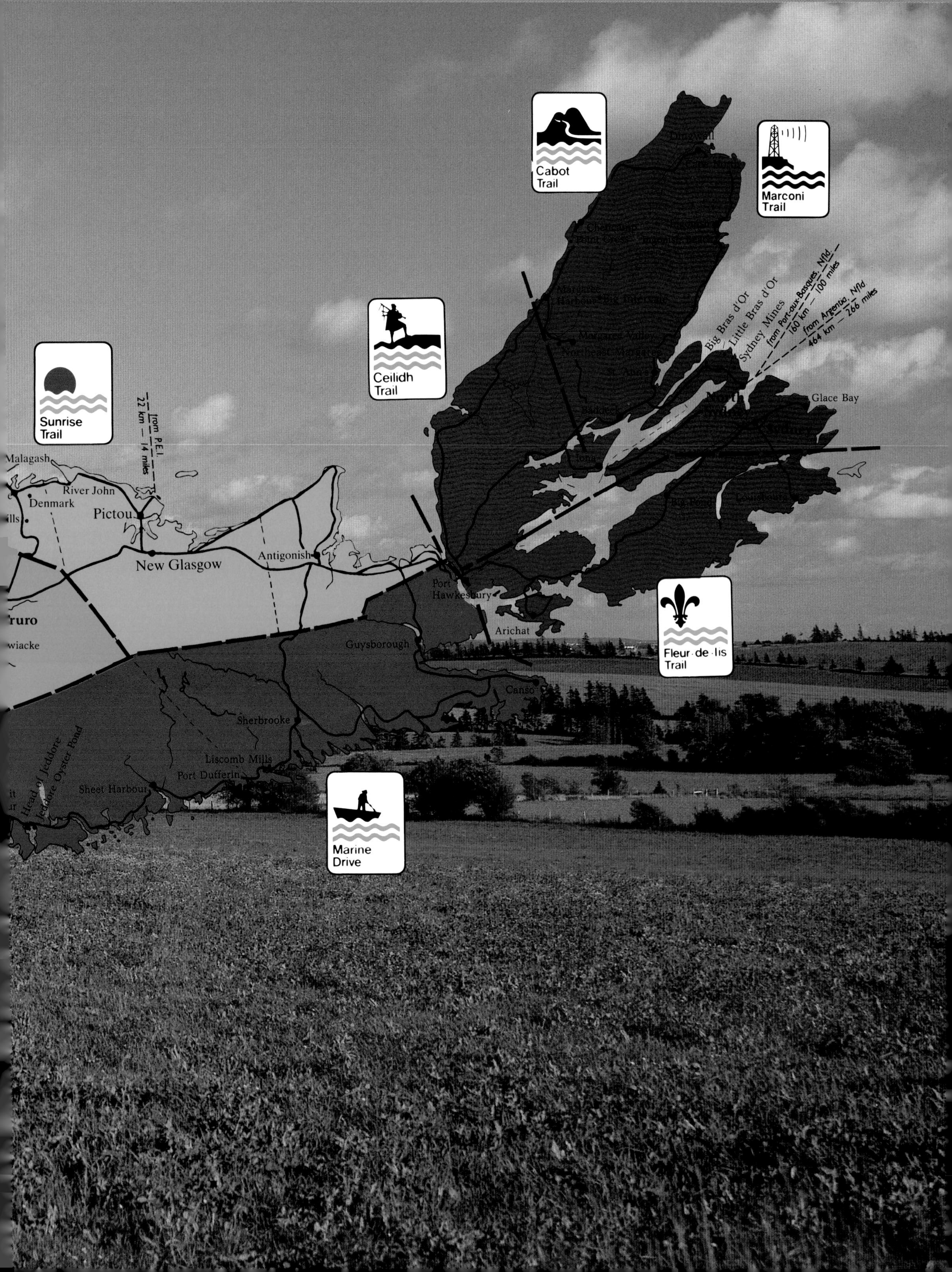
Cabot Trail
Marconi Trail
Ceilidh Trail
Sunrise Trail
Fleur-de-lis Trail
Marine Drive
Big Bras d'Or
Little Bras d'Or
Sydney Mines
from Port-aux-Basques, Nfld
160 km — 100 miles
from Argentia, Nfld
464 km — 266 miles
Glace Bay
from P.E.I.
22 km — 14 miles
Malagash
River John
Denmark
Pictou
New Glasgow
Antigonish
Port Hawkesbury
Arichat
Guysborough
Canso
Sherbrooke
Liscomb Mills
Port Dufferin
Sheet Harbour
Head of Jeddore
Jeddore Oyster Pond

Halifax Public Gardens
Halifax

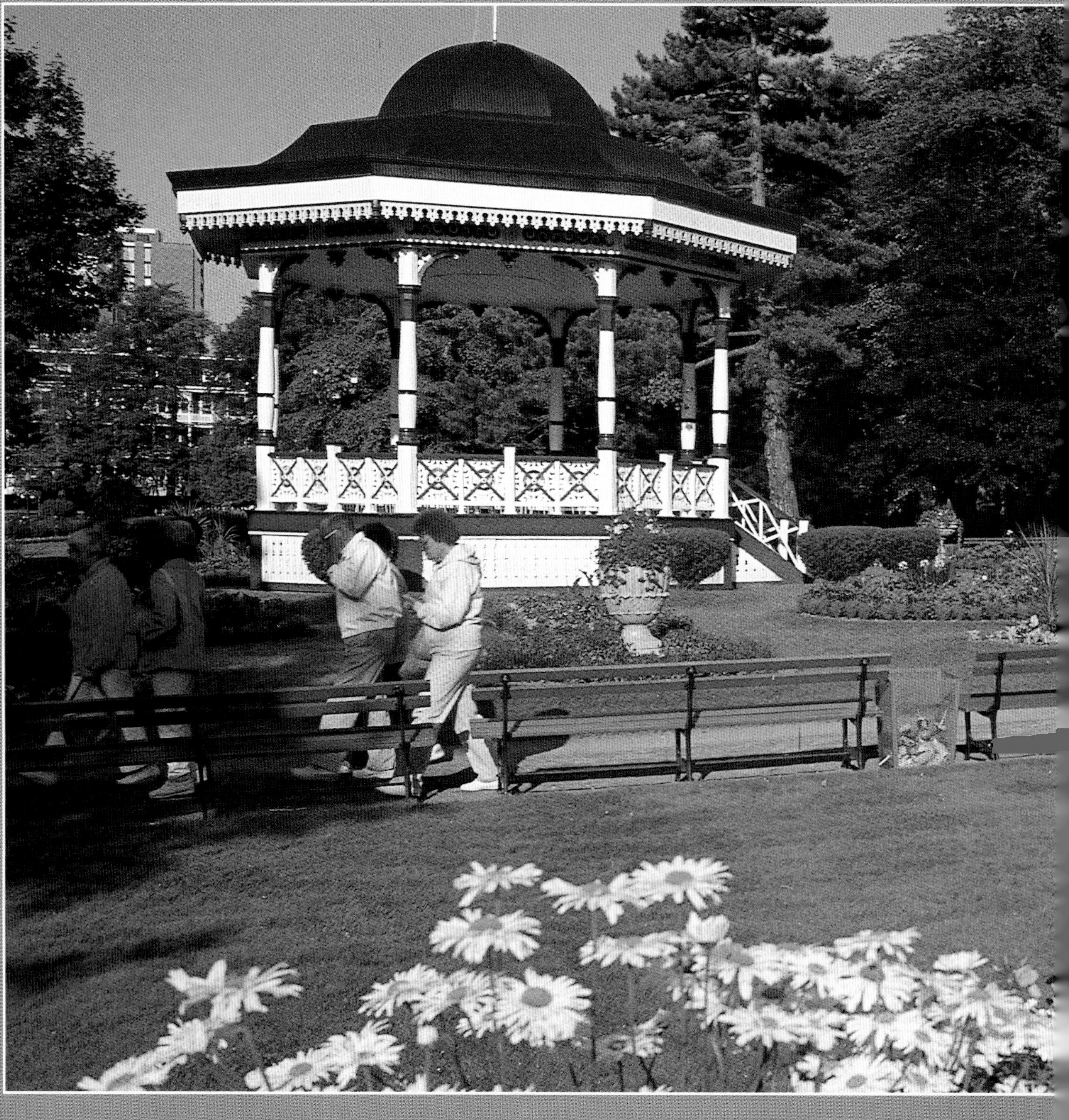

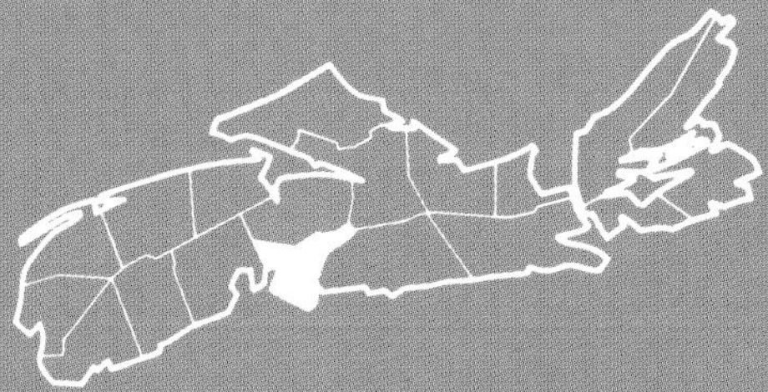

Halifax Dartmouth

BLUENOSE II

Halifax (Below: Halifax Waterfront)

Halifax

Halifax

17

Milton
Queen's County

Lighthouse Route

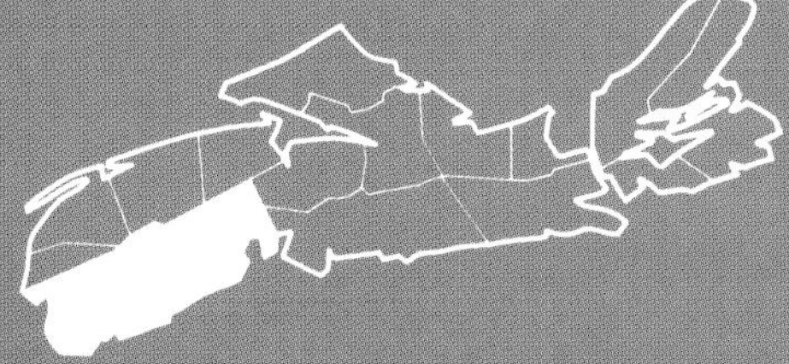

INN-JOY
TEA
ROOM

Beales
Bailiwick
Beales' Bailiwick Ltd.
Suttles and Seawinds
COTTON FASHIONS
H. Barbeau
MOCCASINS
Woof Design
MOHAIR SWEATERS
Beale
T-SHIRTS

Peggy's Cove

Upper Tantallon

The Captain's House
Dining Room and Lounge
Fully Licensed
(1822)

78

Chester

Mahone Bay

ADMIRAL BENBOW
· TRADING COMPANY ·
INTERNATIONAL CODE
Suffolk Smellies
Suffolk Smellies
ADMIRAL BENBOW
OPEN

the
Innlet
café
HADDOCK CHOWDER
CAFÉ

Mahone Bay

Mahone Bay

Suttles
and
Seawinds
Quilts·Clothing·Gifts
Fabrics
466 Main St. Mahone Bay, N.S.

Suttles and Seawinds

Mahone Bay

in
MAHONE BAY
Zwicker's
Inn
LICENSED
RESTAURANT
662 MAIN
"THE FOOD IS SUPERB"
The Zwicker Inn
662

BLUENOSE LODGE
Bluenose
LODGE
VACANCY
Bluenose
LODGE
FINE DINING AND ACCOMMODATION
Breakfast 8:00 - 9:30
Lunch 12:00 - 2:00
Dinner 5:30 - 8:30

Boscawen
Inn

Lunenburg

ART GALLERY

Lunenburg

Lunenburg

Lunenburg

Café
THE GINGER JAR
Food for Health
THE GINGER JAR
THE GINGER JAR

MONTAGUE
WOOLLENS
classic
fashions
Montague Woollens
-Fine clothing -ladies -mens -childrens
MONTAGUE
Gallery
FINE ART
paintings • prints • pottery
Gail Patriarche

Lunenburg

AVOCA-IRISH
MONTAGU
WOOLLEN
classic
fashions
MONTAGUE
MONTAGUE WOOLLENS
classic fashions
Teddy Bear Knits
Gallery FINE ART

C. J. BUCK & Co.
Lunenburg
Outfitters
138

C.J.BUCK & Co.
Lunenburg
Outfitters

Snug Harbour
BED & BREAKFAST
9

The
Lunenburg
Inn
Fine Food
and
Lodging
Fully Licensed
Private Baths

Bridgewater

Petite Riviere

Broad Cove

Liverpool

The Cooper's
INN
RESTAURANT

COUNTRY PINE

TEA ROOM
Toddle In
BED & BREAKFAST
The CURIOSITY SHOPPE

Barrington

Hunt's Point

Barrington Passage

Penney Estate
Ltd.
BED & BREAKFAST
ATKINSON'S

Cape Blomidon
Kings County

Evangeline Trail

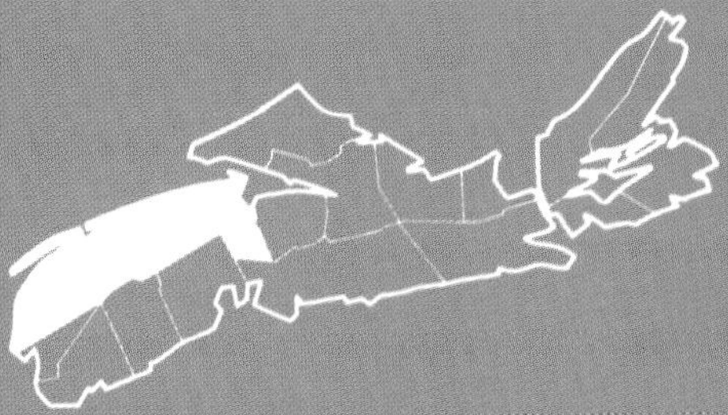

1915
FIREFIGHTERS' MUSEUM
NATIONAL
EXHIBIT
CENTRE
CLOSED

Yarmouth

At the Sign of the Whale
Nova Scotia Cr
Art Gallery
Morris Pottery S
At the Sign of the Whale
NOVA SCOTIA CRAFTS

Meteghan

PINES

Sandy Cove

Sandy Cove

Westport

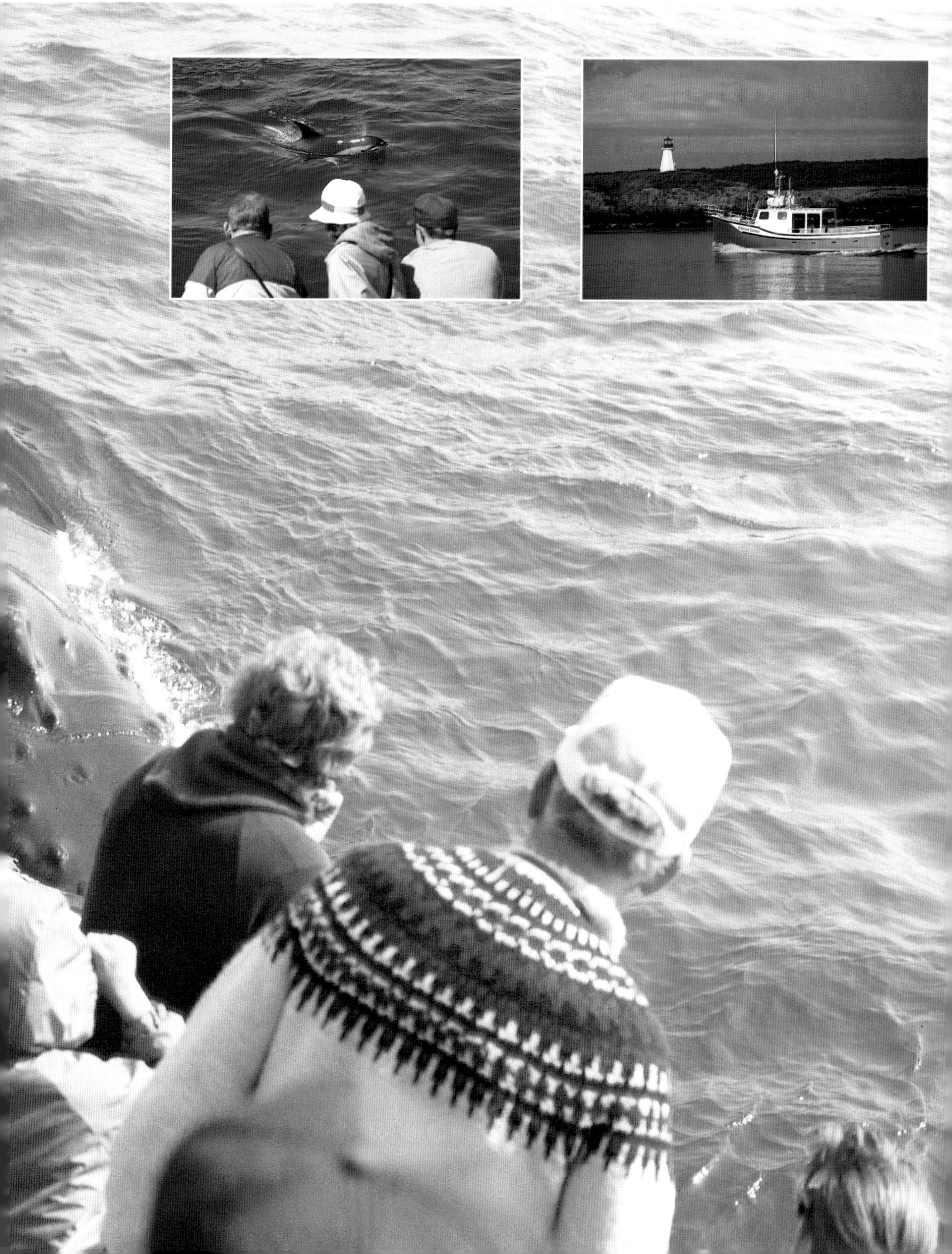

WESTPORT INN
BED & BREAKFAST
NO VACANCY
153

RESTAURANT
RESTAURANT
161
WESTPORT
INN
BED & BREAKFAST
RESTAURANT
GROCERY ITEMS
Home of the...
Briar Island Burger
Good homemade food!
OPEN YEAR AROUND
Ph.839-2675

Westport

Smith's Cove

Smith's Cove

Smith's Cove

Annapolis Royal

Granville Ferry

THE
TOLMIE GALLERY
at Saratoga
FINE ART

Middleton

Broadstreet
Cafe'
Broadstreet
Cafe'
Delicious Food Cozy Atmosphere
WELCOME
PEPSI

127

EXIT

VICTORIA'S
HISTORIC INN & MOTEL
DINING ROOM
DINING HOURS
5:30PM-9:00PM
416
OFFICE
ACCOMMODATIONS

THE WEAVE SHED
Crafts Co-operative Ltd
FINE NOVA SCOTIAN CRAFTS
Nova Scotia
CRAFTS
OPEN

Port Williams

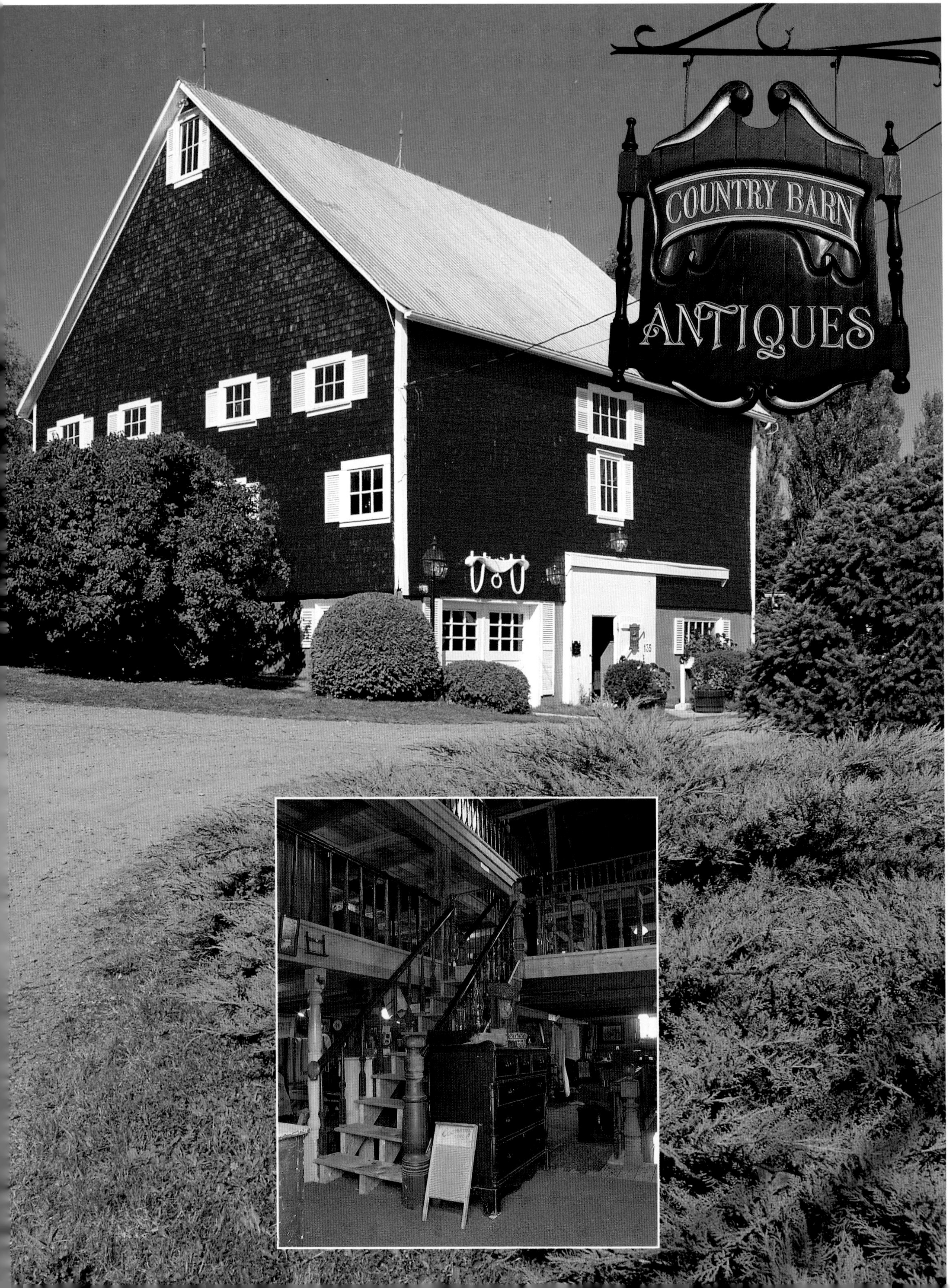

Port Williams

Port Williams

Port Williams

Canning

Canning

Canning

King's County

Poplar Grove
Hants County

Glooscap Trail

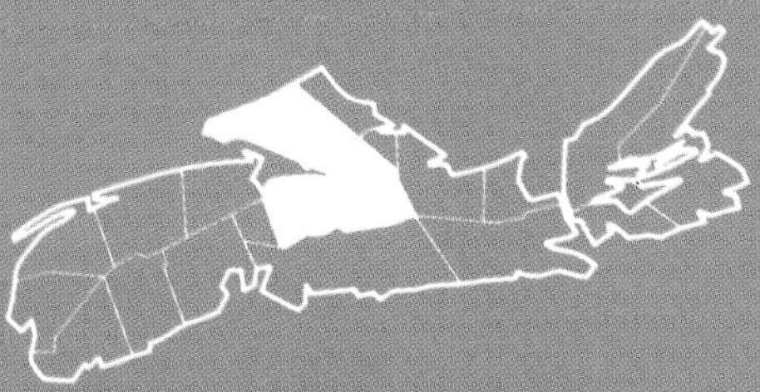

Glooscap Trail

HAGGIS, YA' SAY!!??... WELL OF COUR-R--RSE THA' SERVE HAGGIS, MON!

M/V. KIPAWO

MIRACLE
BLOOD ON THE COAL
BLOOD
ON THE
COAL
MINERS' MUSEUM
SPRINGHILL
NOVA SCOTIA
TOUR A MINE
UNDERGROUND
TOUR A MINE
SPRINGHILL
MINERS MUSEUM

Balmoral Mills
Colchester County

Sunrise Trail

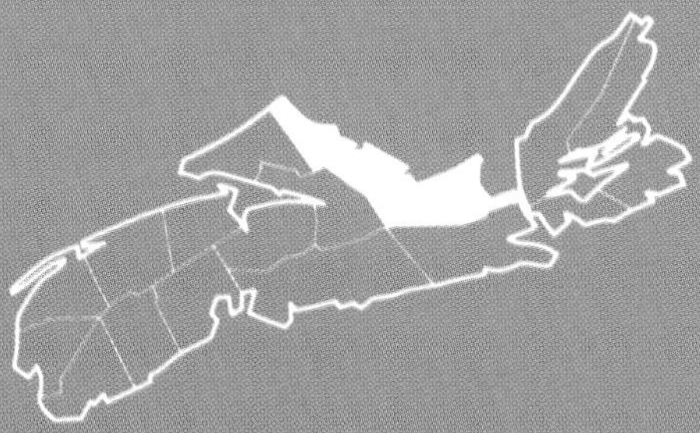

Amherst

CANADIAN STERLING
OPEN

Pugwash

SEAGULL
PEWTERERS & SILVERSMITHS
FINE CRAFTS & ANTIQUES
OPEN

Pugwash

Wallace

SWEATER OUTLET
Cumberland County Knitters
CRAFTS GIFTS SOUVENIRS

TATAMAGOUCHE.

Pictou

Pictou

New Glasgow

Pictou

Cabot Trail
Cape Breton

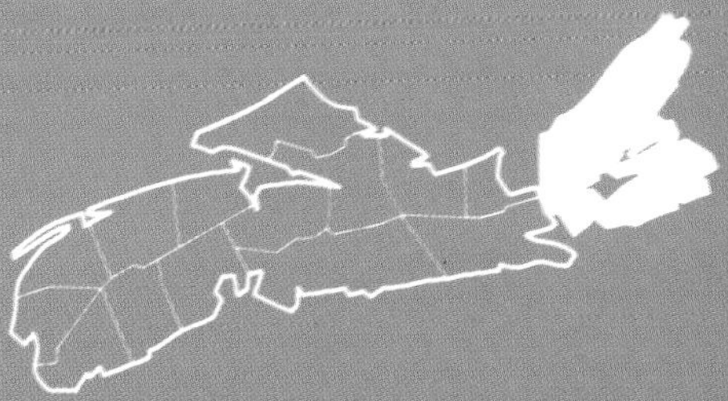

Cape Breton Trails

EFFECTS
DAD

North East Margaree

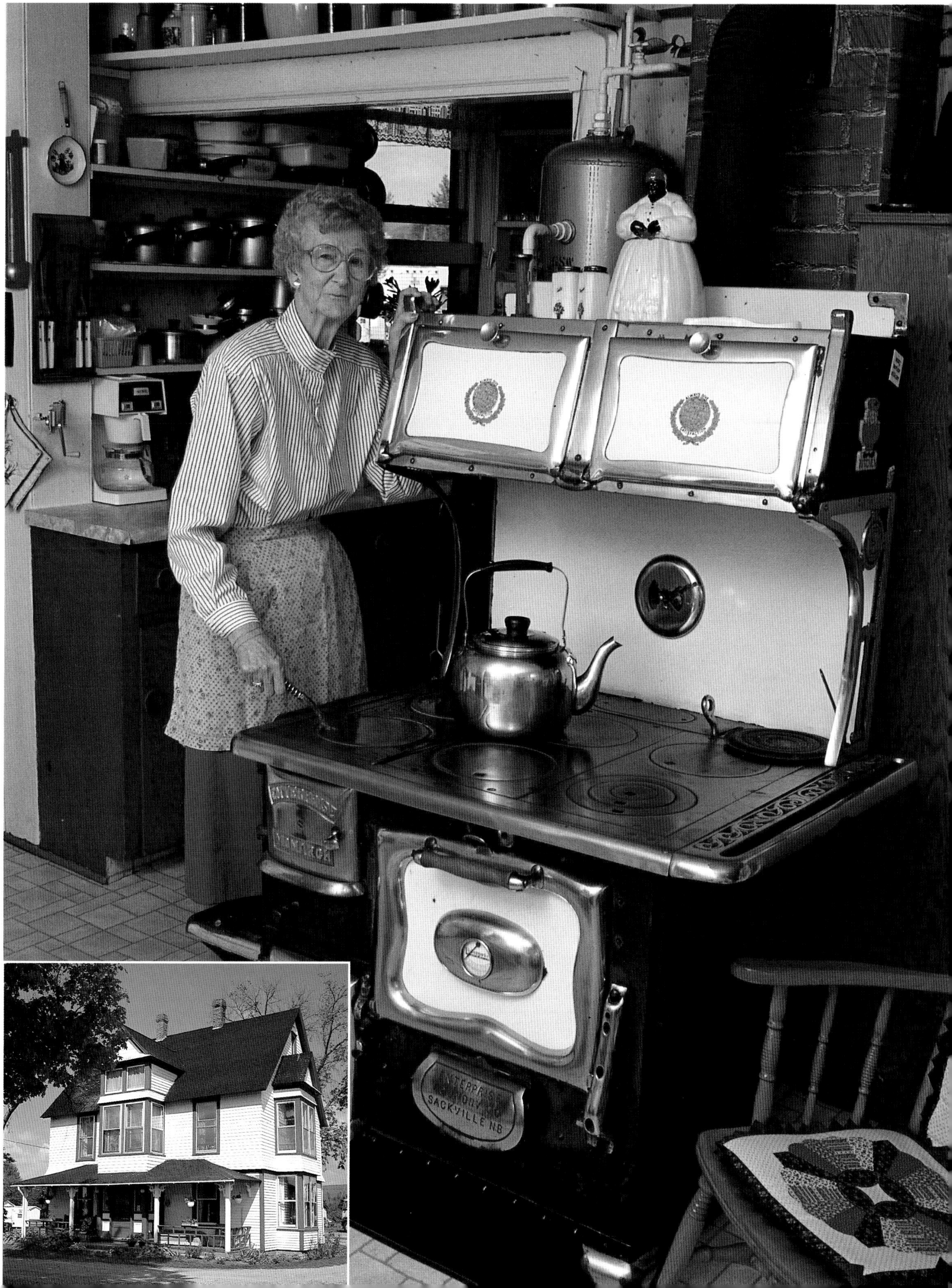

Margaree Valley

FLORA'S
FLORA'S
HANDCRAFTS-ARTISANATS
ICE
CREAM
PARLOR
FLORA'S

Dingwall

Dingwall

Ingonish Beach

Baddeck

SEAWINDS
CHANDLERY

Baddeck

Baddeck

Telegraph House
MOTEL
Dining Room
MEMBER
INNKEEPERS' GUILD OF NOVA SCOTIA

Iona

Iona

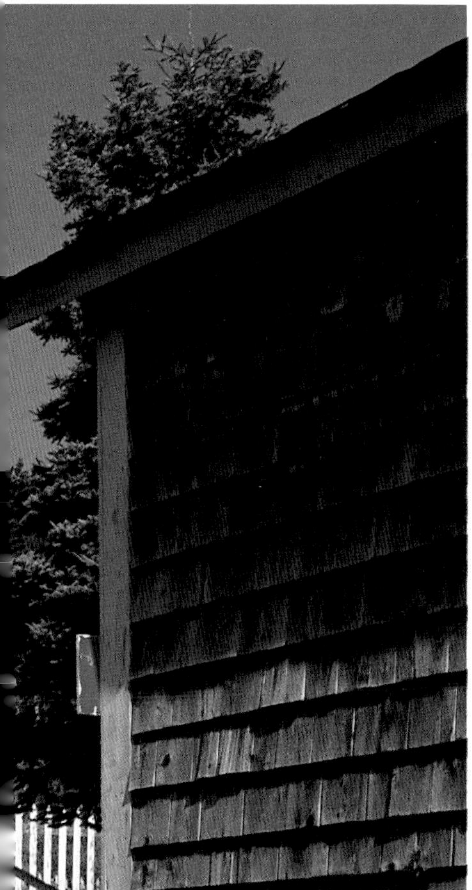

Sydney Mines

Sydney

Cape Breton
Bed
&
Breakfast

CAPE BRETON ISLAND
NOVA SCOTIA'S
MASTERPIECE
Put yourself in the picture!

Sherbrooke Village
Guysborough County

Marine Drive

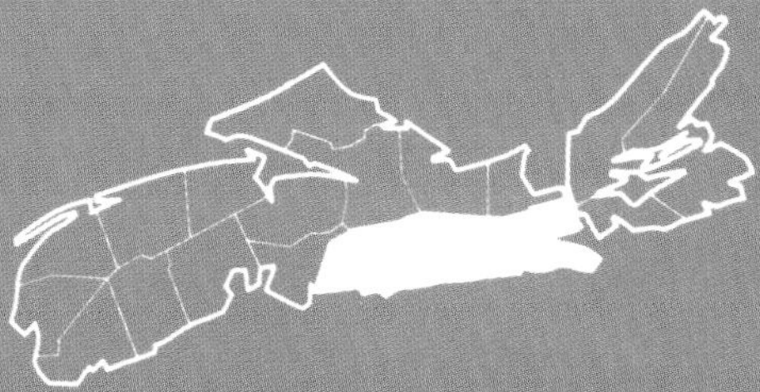

Marine Drive

Marquis of Dufferin
Marquis of Dufferin
Chardonnay

Liscomb Mills

Liscomb Mills

Sherbrooke

Halifax Dartmouth

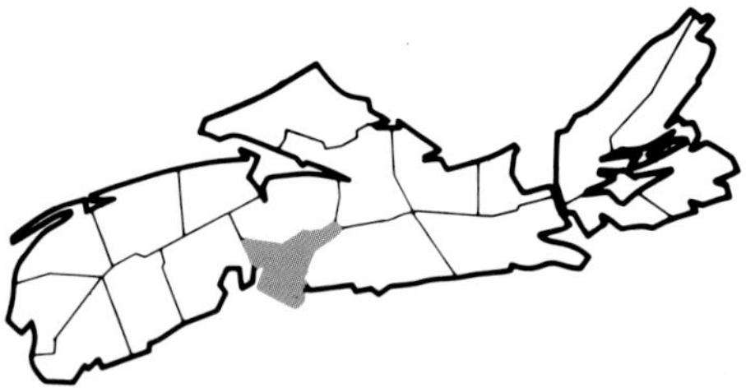

Grade Star Descriptions

★	*Basic, clean, comfortable accommodation*
★★	*Basic, clean, comfortable accommodation with some amenities*
★★★	*Better quality accommodation; greater range of facilities and services*
★★★★	*High quality accommodation; extended range of facilities, amenities and guest services*
★★★★★	*Deluxe accommodation; the greatest range of facilities, amenities and guest services*

- ● Bed & Breakfast
- ▲ Inns
- ♦ Museum/Attraction
- ■ Shop/Gallery
- ✖ Restaurant/Lounge
- ▮ Resort
- ★ Atlantic Canada Accommodations Grading Program

Please Note: All listings appear in alphabetical order.

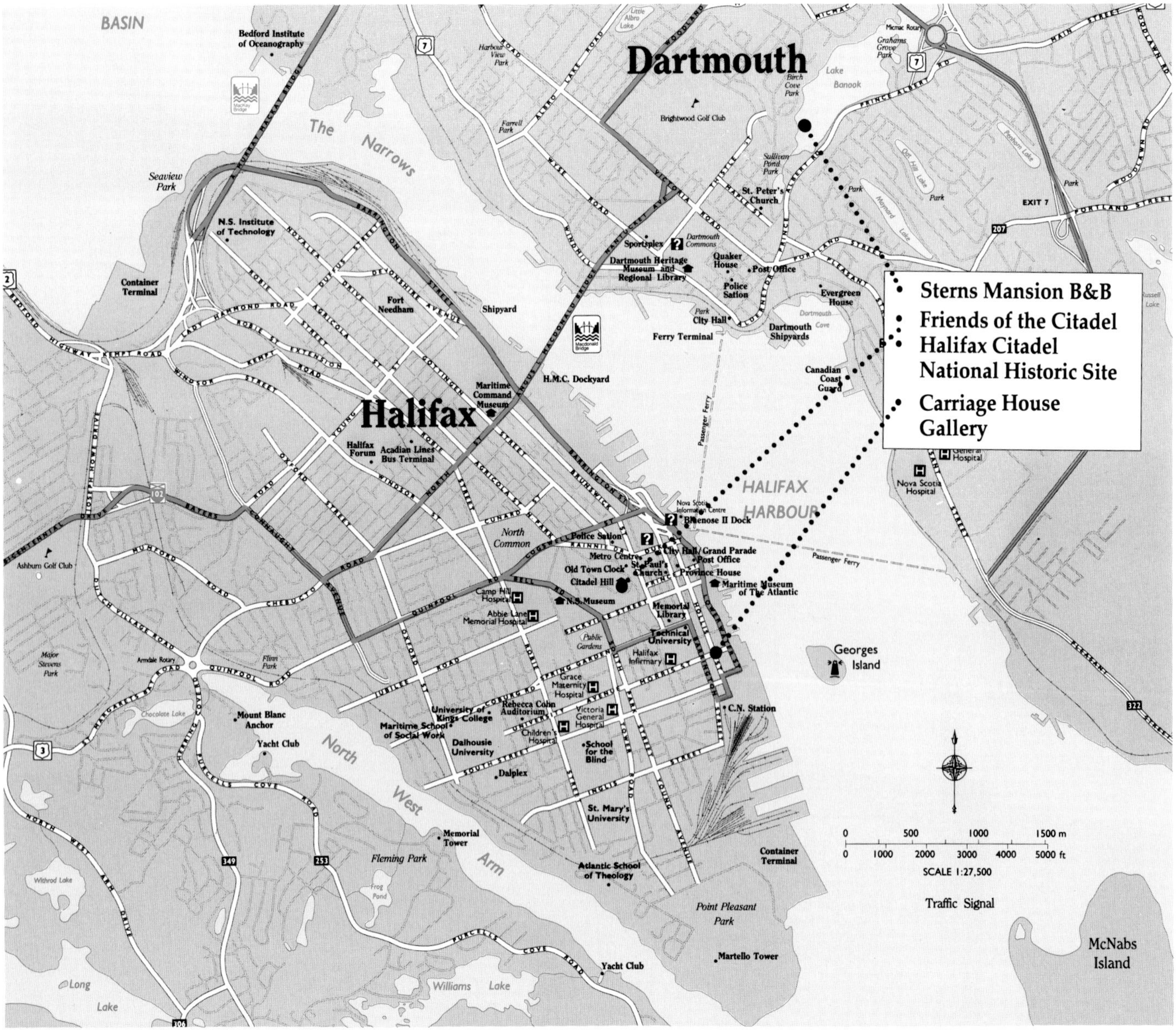

Carriage House Gallery ■
Waterfront Place p. 13
1326 Lower Water Street (at Morris)
Halifax, Nova Scotia B3J 3R3
(902) 425-4482
Located in Waterfront Place (Condominium), the Gallery, with branches in Wolfville and Lunenburg, has earned a reputation for original paintings, prints, fabric art and sculpture by Maritime artists. Call for hours or an appointment.

Friends of the Citadel ■
Box 3116 South p. 14
Halifax, Nova Scotia B3J 3G6
(902) 425-3923
This unusual shop is in the Cavalier Building at the Halifax Citadel National Historic Park. It sells jewellery, books, toys, Victorian Christmas decorations and more, all reflecting the Citadel and life of the period. Proceeds go to supporting the special events and activities of the Friends.

Halifax Citadel National Historic Site ♦
Box 1480, North Postal Station p. 15
Halifax, Nova Scotia B3K 5H7
(902) 426-5080
The Halifax Citadel is situated on a hill overlooking the heart of downtown Halifax. It was constructed between 1828 and 1856 on the site of three previous fortifications, dating to 1749. Today the Halifax Citadel, operated by Environment Canada-Parks, attracts more than one million visitors each year and is recognized as one the most important historical sites in Canada.

Sterns Mansion Bed & Breakfast ▲★
Bill and Holly deMolitor p. 16
17 Tulip Street
Dartmouth, Nova Scotia B3A 2S5
(902) 465-7414
A restored century home in quiet residential area, 6 minutes from downtown Halifax. Antique bedroom suites, brass chandeliers throughout, Victorian decor. 6 rooms private/shared baths, suite with Jacuzzi spa. Candlelight, breakfast, wake-up beverage in room, evening tea, sweets. Wonderful honeymoon packages available. Non-smoking. $55-$100. Year-round. ★★★★ (I/B&B)

Lighthouse Route

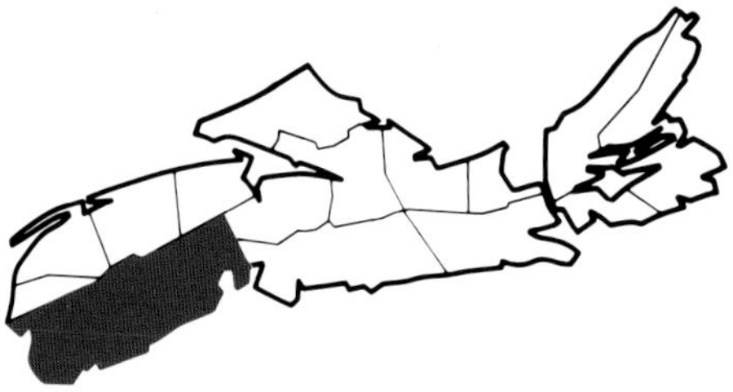

Grade Star Descriptions

★	*Basic, clean, comfortable accommodation*
★★	*Basic, clean, comfortable accommodation with some amenities*
★★★	*Better quality accommodation; greater range of facilities and services*
★★★★	*High quality accommodation; extended range of facilities, amenities and guest services*
★★★★★	*Deluxe accommodation; the greatest range of facilities, amenities and guest services*

- ● Bed & Breakfast
- ▲ Inns
- ♦ Museum/Attraction
- ■ Shop/Gallery
- ✖ Restaurant/Lounge
- ▮ Resort
- ★ Atlantic Canada Accommodations Grading Program

Please Note: All listings appear in alphabetical order.

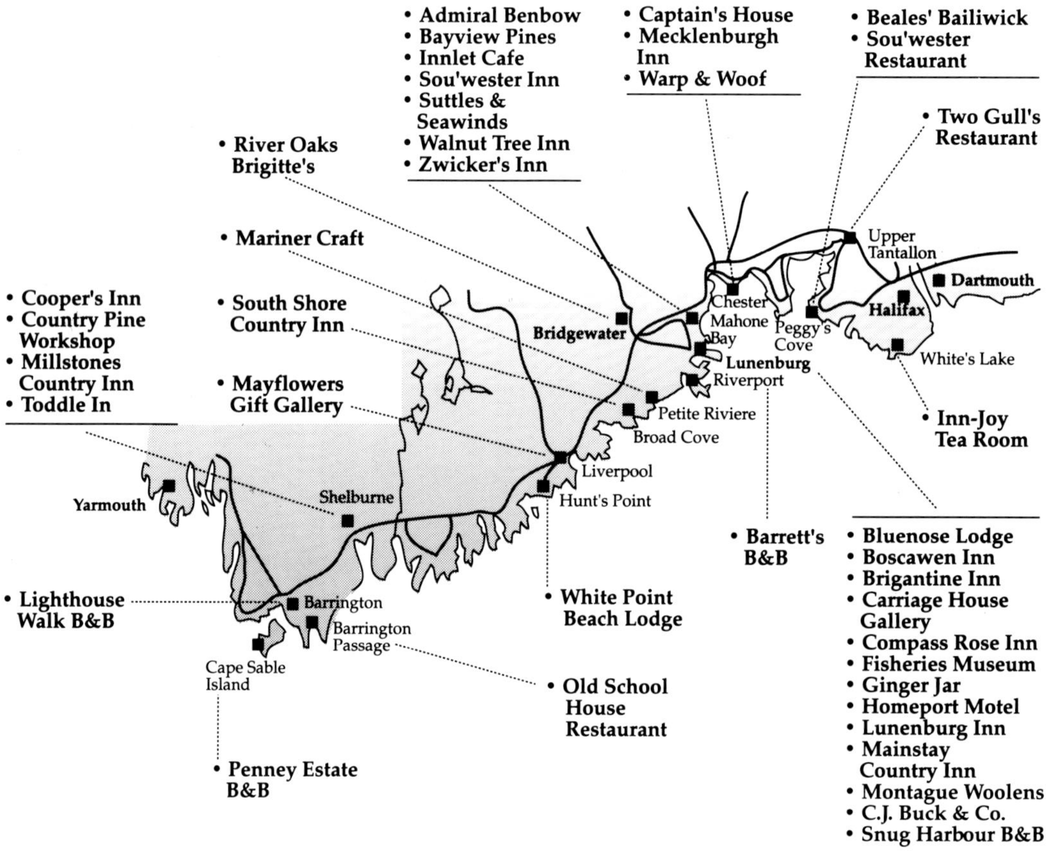

Admiral Benbow Trading Company ■
Paul and Diana Crosland p. 28
Kedy's Landing
Mahone Bay, Nova Scotia B0J 2E0
(902) 624-9033
After a good passage with favourable winds our cargo has been secured and landed. Now in our Lunenburg and Mahone Bay stores you'll find traditional sweaters from Scotland and Wales, the well-known Guernsey, Swiss cotton nightwear for the ladies, Maritime crafts, decorative and practical gifts for the home. Year-round. VISA, M/C.

Barrett's Bed & Breakfast ● ★
Bill and Sheila Barrett p. 51
RR # 1
Riverport, Nova Scotia B0J 2W0
(902) 766-4655
Restored captain's house with 30 acres fronting on Lunenburg Bay. Decorated in country antiques with large country kitchen and breakfast to match. Three rooms with two shared baths. Fishing boat excursions available to guests. 10 minutes west of Lunenburg off Route 332, just past Ovens Park. Year-round. VISA, M/C.
★★★ (I/B&B)

Bayview Pines Country Inn ▲ ★
Curt, Nancy and Steve Norklun p. 27
678 Oakland Road, R.R. 2, Indian Point
Mahone Bay, Nova Scotia B0J 2E0
(902) 624-9970
A charming turn-of-the-century historic farmhouse and converted barn set on 21 acres of pasture and woodland overlooking the Bay. All of our eight guestrooms are decorated with original or period furnishings and have water view. Private baths. "Our Country Kitchen" available for breakfast, lunch and dinner. Year-round. VISA, M/C.
★★★★ (I/B&B)

Beales' Bailiwick ■
John and Fay Beale p. 21
Peggy's Cove, Nova Scotia B0J 2N0
(902) 823-2099
In the traditional fishing village of Peggy's Cove, we offer crafts and art from Nova Scotia and across Canada. We present Suttles and Seawinds cotton fashions, Woof Design mohair sweaters, wares and jewellery from Seagull Pewterers and Silversmiths and our own Beale-designed art T-shirts. Dwell over the view from our deck with coffee bar, May-October. (Year-round at our Halifax International Airport shop.)

Bluenose Lodge ▲ ✖ ★
Ron and Grace Swan p. 35
Corner Falkland and Dufferin Sts.
Box 399
Lunenburg, Nova Scotia B0J 2C0 (902) 634-8851
This 125-year-old mansion has nine rooms, private bathrooms, and is within walking distance of shops, galleries, historic buildings and waterfront of Lunenburg. Local specialties, freshest seafood and sumptuous desserts are offered in our fully licensed restaurant. Complimentary breakfasts feature treats such as fresh muffins, stewed rhubarb and quiche.
★★★★ (I/B&B)

Boscawen Inn ▲ ★
Ann and Michael O'Dowd p. 36
150 Cumberland Street, Box 1343
Lunenburg, Nova Scotia B0J 2C0
(902) 634-3325
Built as a dowry gift in 1888, this wonderful Victorian mansion has 17 bedrooms, small and cosy to large and elegant with sitting areas overlooking the harbour. Attractive dining room serves 3 meals daily, including seafood specialties. Three inviting sitting rooms where fires burn on chilly nights. Spacious deck with panoramic view. $35-$85. Easter to New Year.
★★★ (I/B&B)

Brigantine Inn, Bistro and Coffee Shop ▲ ✖
Jonathan and Merle McCann p. 38
82 Montague Street, Box 1029
Lunenburg, Nova Scotia B0J 2C0
(902) 634-3300
The inn has seven beautifully appointed and individually decorated rooms, several overlooking the harbour and golf course, one with private balcony. All have 4-piece baths. The guest sitting room with private balcony also overlooks the harbour. The fully licensed, wheelchair-accessible bistro and coffee shop offering a wide array of maritime fare and desserts is open to the public. Year-round.

The Captain's House Restaurant ✖
Nicky Butler p. 24
129 Central Street
Chester, Nova Scotia B0J 1J0 (902) 275-3501
Dating from 1822, the house was once home of Rev. John Seccombe, one of Chester's first settlers. Today its fully licensed dining room, bar and patio, overlooking the ocean, offer morning coffee, lunch, afternoon tea, full-scale evening dining and Sunday brunch. Comprehensive menu includes traditional Nova Scotia specialties and fine wines. Wharf for marine travellers. Wheelchair accessible. Complimentary sunsets.

Carriage House Gallery ■
Capitol Theatre p. 40
290 Lincoln Street
Lunenburg, Nova Scotia B0J 2C0
(902) 634-4010 or 634-8094
A former Oddfellows Hall, built on nautical principles by shipwrights, the accoustically brilliant Capitol Theatre Arts Centre and Opera House still displays its original curved stage and footlights. In the Great Hall high above the Opera House you'll find the Carriage House Gallery, renowned for its original works by Maritime artists. Gallery branches also in Wolfville and Halifax. Call for hours or an appointment.

C.J. Buck & Co. ■
John and Gail Patriarche p. 48
138 Montague St., Box 1600
Lunenburg, Nova Scotia B0J 2C0
(902) 634-4334
Rugged outdoor and casual clothing for the whole family, that is wearable, washable, lovable and relaxing. Well-known names such as Tilley, Koolah, GWG, R.G. Brown, Canadian Wilderness Outfitters. Chamois shirts, the famous Lunenburg jackets, sweaters, oiled jackets and coats from Australia and a unique line of company T-shirts, sweats, golf shirts, tank tops and more.

The Compass Rose Inn and Dining Room ▲ ✖ ★
Rodger and Suzanne Pike p. 41
15 King Street, Box 1267
Lunenburg, Nova Scotia B0J 2C0 (902) 634-8509
This heritage property, circa 1825, is a fine example of Georgian architecture. The inn features five comfortable rooms with private baths. The licensed dining rooms specialize in fresh seafoods, steaks, local dishes and mouth-watering desserts. A cozy lounge and an outdoor garden offer respite to the weary traveller. Complimentary breakfast. Open daily for breakfast, lunch and dinner. VISA, M/C, AMX, EnRoute.
★★★ (I/B&B)

The Cooper's Inn and Restaurant ▲ ★
Gary and Cynthia Hynes p. 56
36 Dock Street, Box 959
Shelburne, Nova Scotia B0T 1W0 (902) 875-4656
An elegantly restored 1785 home furnished with antiques, this country inn offers guestrooms with private baths and water views. Its licensed dining room is noted for quality cuisine served in an ambience of ocean views, candlelight and friendly hospitality. Located harbourside, just steps from the tourist bureau. Rooms include breakfast. Supper 5:30-9:00 daily, May-Oct. VISA, M/C, AMX.
★★★ (I/B&B)

The Country Pine Workshop ■
Nancy and Lawrence Mahaney p. 57
Hwy 103, Box 1030
Shelburne, Nova Scotia B0T 1W0
(902) 875-3200
This large gift shop is surrounded by gardens and features an active and complete woodworking shop. Stock includes a range of Nova Scotia crafts along with the owners' own wood-working and Northern dufflework. On Hwy 103, 1/4 mile east of exit 25 to Shelburne.

Fisheries Museum of the Atlantic ♦
Nova Scotia Museum Complex p. 42
Box 1363, Route 3
Lunenburg, Nova Scotia B0J 2C0
(902) 634-4794
Visitors welcomed wharfside aboard two former deep-sea fishing vessels. The buildings house an aquarium, three floors of exhibits, a theatre and a working dory shop. The exhibits include a history of the famous Bluenose and the story of rum-running. Gift shop and restaurant. May 15-Oct 15; 9:30-5:30 daily. Admission charge.

The Ginger Jar Natural Foods & Cafe ✖ ■
Marnie Clark p. 43
251 Lincoln Street, Box 1528
Lunenburg, Nova Scotia B0J 2C0
(902) 634-4000
Enjoying and appreciating personal contact with customers is our special touch. We offer a wide variety of natural bulk foods, macrobiotic and Chinese cuisine items, vitamins, herbs and spices, books, home-made breads and ice creams. Delicious healthy lunches served daily. Pitas, salads, sandwiches, bagels, scones and muffins. Mon-Sat 9:00-5:30; Sun (July & Aug)1:00-5:00. Welcome friends.

Homeport Motel ▲
167 Victoria Road, Box 1510 p. 45
Lunenburg, Nova Scotia B0J 2C0
Phone/Fax (902) 634-8234
Large motel rooms with twin double beds. New "executive suites" with double and queen size beds, living room with hide-a-bed, full kitchen with microwave, fridge, stove, dishwasher, dining area, large corner whirlpool tubs; also large two bedroom housekeeping unit available; air-conditioning, phone, Maritime style meals, conference room, honeymoon package. $85-$125. Year-round.

Inn-Joy Tea Room and Bed & Breakfast ● ✖
Joyce and Jerry Platz p. 20
3505 Prospect Road, White's Lake, R.R. 4
Armdale, N.S. B3L 4J4
(902) 852-2543
A bit of the "Old Country" Nova Scotia style. Drop in for breakfast or lunch and "Inn-Joy" fresh-from-the-oven scones, muffins and fruit crisps in our cozy tea room. Ample parking and wheelchair accessible. June-Sept 8-4. Closed Mondays. 2 rooms, double beds, private baths, complete breakfast incl. Double $45, Single $30.

The Innlet Cafe ✖
Jack Sorenson p. 29
Kedy's Landing
Mahone Bay, Nova Scotia B0J 2E0
(902) 624-6363
A casual but stylish seaside cafe, grill and seafood house overlooking the famous view of Mahone Bay's three churches. The modestly priced, all-day menu includes grilled fish, chowders and soups, sandwiches, burgers, steaks, stir-fries, salads, breakfast items, muffins and specialty desserts. Licensed. Exit 10 or 11 from Hwy 103. Open daily 10 - 8. Apr-Dec. VISA, M/C.

Lighthouse Walk Bed & Breakfast ● ★
Emma Kennedy p. 60
Box 156
Barrington, Nova Scotia B0W 1E0
(902) 637-3409
A restored 17-room Georgian heritage home once known as MacMullen Hotel. Large windows with ocean view, plants, antique wicker, oak and collections in the keeping room encourage gatherings. 45 min. east of Yarmouth, next to the Barrington Lighthouse, Old Meeting House and Woollen Mill Museums. Single $30; Double $35-$40. June 1-Sept 30.
★★★ (I/B&B)

The Lunenburg Inn ✖ ▲ ★
John and Faith Piccolo p. 50
26 Dufferin Street, Box 1407
Lunenburg, Nova Scotia B0J 2C0
(902) 634-3963
This turn-of-the-century home recalls the charm of yesteryear – but the plumbing is of today. All rooms have private baths and are furnished with antiques and collectibles. The loft suite includes a whirlpool bath and kitchen. Complimentary full breakfast. The licensed restaurant offers fresh Nova Scotia seafood and authentic Mediterranean cuisine. Recommended in *Where to Eat in Canada*. Year-round. ★★★ (I/B&B)

The Mainstay Country Inn ● ★
Pierre and Nancy Dion p. 44
167 Victoria Road, Box 1510
Lunenburg, Nova Scotia B0J 2C0
Phone/Fax (902) 634-8234
This beautiful estate (circa 1853) is the former home of Senator William Duff. Splendid rooms with antiques and country decor. Private baths with whirlpool tubs. Honeymoon suite with canopy bed. One suite with fridge and stove. Continental/full breakfasts and Maritime style meals. $47-$65. Year-round. Next to Save Easy Food market.
★★★ (I/B&B)

Mariner Craft ■
Kim and Steve McKenzie p. 53
R.R. 1
Petite Riviere, Nova Scotia B0J 2P0
(902) 688-2667
Built in 1892 as a general store, the Mariner Craft retains its original flavour. Situated in picturesque Petite Riviere (founded in 1632), it is close to an antique shop, a restaurant, a general store and beaches, including Rissers Beach Provincial Park. Features Nova Scotia handcrafts, including sagged bubble glass, leather goods and jewellery made on premises. Easter to mid-December

Mayflowers Gift Gallery ■
Robin Gale Williams p. 55
22 Market Street
Liverpool, Nova Scotia B0T 1K0
(902) 354-2809
Mayflowers, in this historic seaport, combines the best of Nova Scotia crafts with innovative country and Victorian decorating ideas. Located off Main Street, it has nooks and alcoves filled with exciting treasures – pottery, pewter, decorator prints and Nova Scotia-crafted jewellery. The atmosphere is potpourri-filled and browsers are welcome. Year-round.

Mecklenburgh Inn ●
Suzan Fraser p. 25
78 Queen Street, Box 350
Chester, Nova Scotia B0J 1J0
(902) 275-4638
Built in 1890 and operated as a hat shop for many years, the inn is centrally located and minutes from the ocean. Guests will enjoy a gourmet breakfast served in gracious surroundings, prepared by Sue Fraser who was trained at the London Cordon Bleu school. June 1-Sept 30. VISA

The Millstones Country Inn ▲ ✖ ● ★
Shirley Guthridge p. 58
2 Falls Lane, Box 758
Shelburne, Nova Scotia B0T 1W0 (902) 875-3958
Relax on our large porch and admire the old millstones incorporated in the front access of this inn located 5 min. from historic Dock Street. 3 B&B bedrooms with private baths. One family suite (sleeps up to 5) with private bath. Close to swimming, walking and Islands Provincial Park. The fully licensed, wheelchair accessible dining room, seating 34, is open to the public, incl small parties, for lunch and dinner. VISA. ★★★ (I/B&B)

Montague Woollens, Montague Gallery ■
John and Gail Patriarche p. 46
3 King Street, Box 1600
Lunenburg, Nova Scotia B0J 2C0
(902) 634-4333
Beautifully fashioned hand-woven capes, jackets, suits, blankets, throws and tartans, classic ladies' wear. Fantastic selection of designer and classic sweaters of wool, mohair, cotton – men's and ladies'. See the famous Guernsey yachting sweater. In the Gallery: new selection of watercolours and limited-edition prints by artist Gail Patriarche.

The Old School House Restaurant ✖
Route 3, Box 587 p. 62
Barrington Passage, Nova Scotia B0W 1G0
(902) 637-3770
You'll find a warm and friendly welcome along with quality food and service at The Old School House. Fresh charbroiled fish is our specialty. Delicious salads, fresh fruit pies and daily specials complete our menu. A memorable atmosphere is created by hand-hewn beams, unique shanties and a fieldstone fireplace. June 1- Sept 30, 10 -10; Oct 1 - May 31, 10 - 9. Closed Saturdays. VISA.

Penney Estate Bed & Breakfast ●
Lois and Hubbie Atkinson p. 64
Box 57, Barrington Passage, Nova Scotia B0W 1G0
(902) 745-1516 or 745-3359
This turn-of-the-century home has been completely restored and renovated to meet modern standards and offers excellent, comfortable accommodations for a peaceful overnight stay. Secluded beach. Cable TV in all rooms. Located in Northeast Point, Cape Sable Island, just 45 min. from Yarmouth. From Rte 103, cross causeway to Cape Sable Island, turn left at N.E. Point/Clam Point intersection. Inquire for handicapped facilities. Year-round.

River Oaks ● ■
Brigitte's Bed & Breakfast p. 52
Brigitte Butzow
312 LaHave Street
Bridgewater, Nova Scotia B4V 2T7 (902) 543-1743
Relax under oak trees in this lovely old home and cape house on the LaHave River. Browse in the craft and gift shop. Short drive to beaches, historic sites and museums. Close to dining and shopping. 1 double, 1 double plus sofa bed, shared bath, air conditioning. 1 queen in cape house. Guest lounge with TV. Choice of three breakfasts included. No smoking please. Double $45, Queen $55. VISA, M/C.

Snug Harbour Bed & Breakfast ●
Nancy Callen p. 49
9 King Street, Box 1390
Lunenburg, Nova Scotia B0J 2C0
(902) 634-9146 Fax 634-3019
This century-old home is seen in numerous Canadian calendars and on the back of the one-hundred-dollar bill! It features a third floor sundeck that offers Lunenburg's best view of the harbour. TV and VCR in guest sitting room. Full breakfast. Exit 10 or 11 on Hwy 103.

South Shore Country Inn ▲✖■★
Avril Betts p. 54
Broad Cove, Lunenburg County, Nova Scotia B0J 2H0
(902) 677-2042
Take Hwy 103, Exit 15 from Halifax, Exit 17 from Yarmouth; follow Broad Cove and Inn signs. A stylish, comfortable, four-star English country inn. 6 bedrooms with 3 full semi-private baths, a quaint store and delightful tearoom serving all meals. Beautifully decorated and renovated. 2 min. walk to beach. Ideal for rest and relaxation, honeymooners, hikers, cyclists etc. $42 single, $55 double/twin includes full breakfast. All cards. ★★★★ (I/B&B)

Sou'wester Inn Bed & Breakfast ●★
Ron and Mabel Redden p. 30
788 Main Street, Box 146
Mahone Bay, Nova Scotia B0J 2E0
(902) 624-9296
This seaside shipbuilder's home offers friendly, quiet, gracious accommodations. Four rooms, one with private bath. Verandah overlooking bay. Day-touring/hiking maps. Parlour games, books, tapes, piano. Complimentary evening tea. Nautical gifts including fine whale sculptures. $48-53 couple. May-Oct. VISA, M/C. ★★★★ (I/B&B)

Sou'wester Restaurant and Gift Shop ■✖
Peggy's Cove, Nova Scotia B0J 2N0 p. 22
(902) 823-2561
This family restaurant (with its family prices) is a popular year-round refuge from the breezes of internationally famous Peggy's Cove. Delicious home-style cooking using fresh local fish and vegetables; gingerbread, strawberry and blueberry desserts a specialty. In-house bakery. Panoramic view of St. Margaret's Bay. 10 a.m. to sunset. Closed Christmas Eve, Christmas Day.

Suttles and Seawinds ■
466 Main Street p. 32
Mahone Bay, Nova Scotia B0J 2E0
(902) 624-6177 - Mahone Bay
(902) 644-3110 - New Germany
Vicki Lynn Bardon has won international acclaim for designing fantasy clothing, world-famous quilts, gifts, fashion and home accessories, table linen, children's clothing – all distinctive in colour and design. In Mahone Bay, New Germany or at the Halifax Sheraton. Ask our staff what "suttles" are! Open year-round.

Toddle In Bed & Breakfast and Tearoom ●✖■
Tony Caruso p. 59
Box 837
Shelburne, Nova Scotia B0T 1W0
(902) 875-3229
This 150-year-old Loyalist house is located just steps from the harbour, tourist bureau and surrounding historical buildings. Guest rooms, some with private, others with shared baths, are furnished with period antiques. Sundeck. Attached tearoom is wheelchair accessible. Curiosity shop features handcrafts and Christmas items all year. Open year-round. VISA, M/C.

Two Gulls Restaurant ✖
Anne Dorey p. 23
5250 Bay Road, Upper Tantallon
Box 889A
Halifax, Nova Scotia B3K 5M5
(902) 826-7769
Enjoy the friendly relaxed atmosphere in our licensed, 52-seat dining room and tearoom. The menu features delicious home-style meals at family prices and a wide selection of freshly baked breads and desserts from our own ovens. Private seating for 30 available. Located at Route 3 and Peggy's Cove turn-off. Open year-round. VISA, M/C.

The Walnut Tree Inn ●
Wally and Olga Warren, F.H.C.I.M.A. p. 31
35 Claremont Street, Box 138
Mahone Bay, Nova Scotia B0J 2E0
(902) 624-8039
A little bit of "Brit": the home of retired British hoteliers (England and Jersey, Channel Islands). They offer two double rooms with 1 1/2 shared baths. Complimentary tea and coffee makings in the rooms. Adjacent to swimming pool, tennis court, park, country walks, shopping. Cable T.V. Full English breakfast. Ici on parle français.

The Warp and Woof Gifts & Gallery Limited ■
Anne Flinn p. 26
Water Street, Box 415
Chester, Nova Scotia B0J 1J0
(902) 275-4795
The oldest continuing seasonal gift shop in Nova Scotia opened in 1920, offering quality handcrafts, the work of Nova Scotia artists and the unusual in fine gift items from around the world, a tradition continued today with pride. Main building features pine interior, cathedral ceiling and fine oak railing. May 24-Oct 20.

White Point Beach Lodge ▮
c/o Hunt's Point P.O. p. 61
Hunt's Point, Nova Scotia B0T 1G0
(902) 354-2711/ 1-800-565-5068; Fax (902) 354-7278
Established 1928. Atlantic Canada's oldest privately owned seaside resort. A mile of white sand ocean beach. Rustic log cottages with fireplaces and lodge rooms. Full-service dining and licensed lounge. Magnificent ocean views and beachstone fireplaces. Golf, tennis, indoor and outdoor pools, spa, recreation centre and children's programs. Boating and fishing on-site. Many guests have been returning for generations. Year-round.

Zwicker's Inn (Restaurant) ✖
Iain and Jennifer Hagreen p. 34
622 Main Street, Box 39
Mahone Bay, Nova Scotia B0J 2E0
(902) 624-8045
Zwicker's operated as an inn from 1805-1900 and was refurbished in 1980 as a restaurant. A varied menu specializing in seafood chowder, fresh fish, lobster, lemon steamed mussels, steaks, pork and chicken. Everything, including our noodles, breads and ice creams, is freshly made on the premises. Open daily for lunch 11:30-5:00 and dinner 5:00-9:30. Seats 60. Fully licensed.

Grade Star Descriptions

★	*Basic, clean, comfortable accommodation*
★★	*Basic, clean, comfortable accommodation with some amenities*
★★★	*Better quality accommodation; greater range of facilities and services*
★★★★	*High quality accommodation; extended range of facilities, amenities and guest services*
★★★★★	*Deluxe accommodation; the greatest range of facilities, amenities and guest services*

- ● Bed & Breakfast
- ▲ Inns
- ♦ Museum/Attraction
- ■ Shop/Gallery
- ✖ Restaurant/Lounge
- ▮ Resort
- ★ Atlantic Canada Accommodations Grading Program

Please Note: All listings appear in alphabetical order.

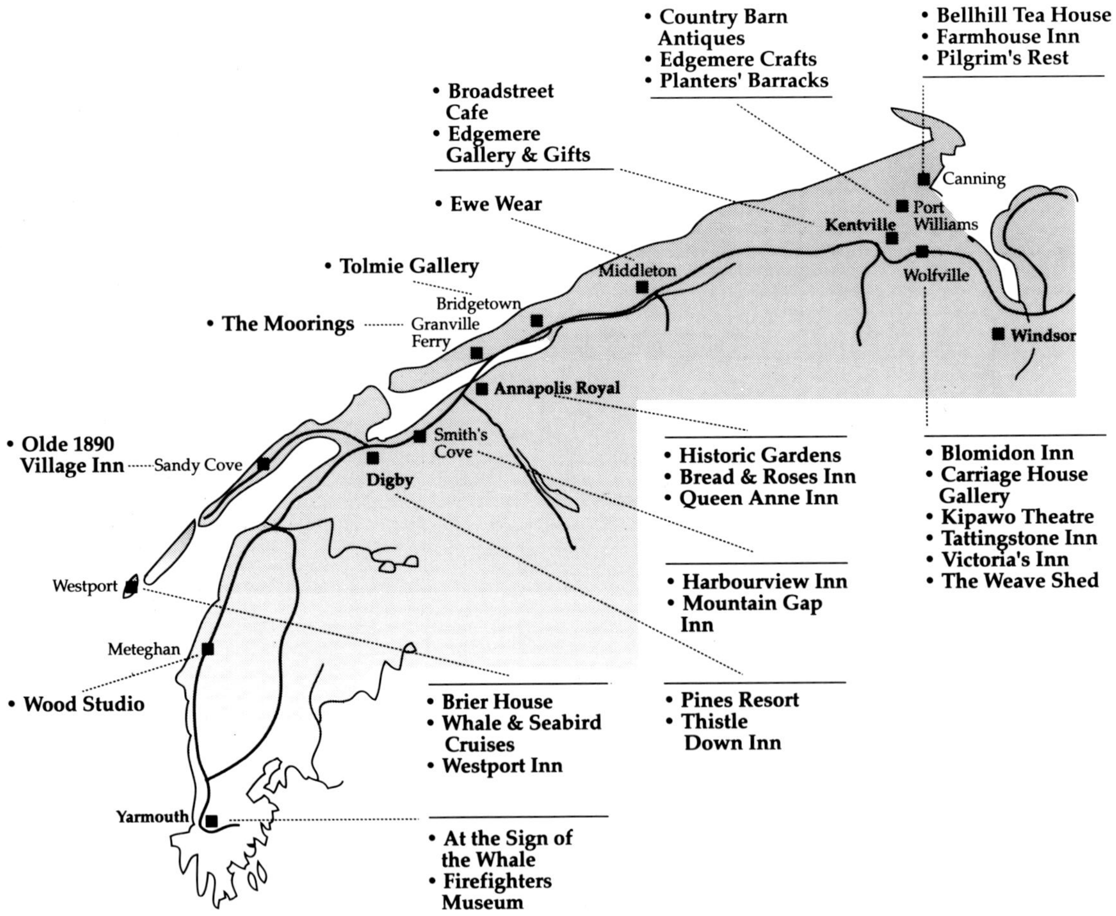

Annapolis Royal Historic Gardens and Restaurant ✖ ♦ p. 86
441 St. George Street, Box 278
Annapolis Royal, Nova Scotia B0S 1A0
(902) 532-7018
Take a relaxing stroll down the winding pathways through 10 acres of picturesque theme gardens, collections and displays reflecting the history of the area. Enjoy fine dining in one of the elegant Victorian dining rooms, sheltered gazebo or outdoor patio. Daily. May-Oct.

At the Sign of the Whale ■ p. 69
Frances and Michael Morris
Box 1040, R.R.1
Yarmouth, Nova Scotia B5A 4A5
(902) 742-8895
Located 2 1/2 miles from Yarmouth on Route 1. 100% quality Nova Scotia crafts and art: Morris pottery made on the premises, driftwood and whale sculptures, scrimshaw, weaving, smocking, one-of-a-kind children's knits, jewellery, glass, pewter, rugs. Original oils, watercolours, art prints by prominent Nova Scotia artists. Year-round. VISA, M/C, AMX.

Bellhill Tea House and Gift Shop ✖ ■ p. 106
Wilma Gibson
Box 35
Canning, Nova Scotia B0P 1H0
(902) 582-7922
From early spring to first day of winter – fresh foods in season prepared and served with care, from fiddle-head quiche, asparagus souffle, raspberry cheesecake to quince jelly, tourtière and rich fruitcake. Sunday brunch, Christmas buffet. Gifts from around the world. Verandah shaded by ancient elms. Bird list – 130+ species.

Blomidon Inn ▲ ★ p. 94
Donna and Jim Laceby
127 Main Street
Wolfville, Nova Scotia B0P 1X0
(902) 542-2291, Fax 542-7461
Offering the gracious comforts of a 19th century sea captain's mansion. Two dining rooms with period furnishings serve local offerings from the Valley and the Sea. Enjoy the tennis court, shuffleboard and large landscaped grounds. In 1990, a modern meeting facility was opened in an adjacent and older sea captain's house. Rates $49-$99 double. Year-round. ★★★★ (I/B&B)

Bread & Roses Country Inn ● p. 88
Don and Jeannie Allen
82 Victoria Street, Box 177
Annapolis Royal, Nova Scotia B0S 1A0
(902) 532-5727
This Victorian brick mansion fulfills the idea that people deserve beauty and inspiration as well as the essentials. Well-appointed, with stained-glass windows, fireplaces. Country breakfast; afternoon and evening tea in the drawing room. No smoking please. $50 single; $65 double; $70 twin; $10 each additional. Nine rooms with private bath. Year-round.

The Brier House ● p. 82
Claire Leng
399 Water Street, Westport
Brier Island, Nova Scotia B0V 1H0 (902) 839-2879
Watch migrating birds and whales from the large deck of this older home overlooking Grand Passage. Ideal location for hiking, photography, hunting rocks, wild flowers and rare plants. 2 rooms with two double beds and cot, 1 room with double and single beds. Shared bathroom. Breakfast included, other meals by request. Rte 217 W from Digby to Westport. Ferry runs every two hours around clock. June 1-Oct 31. Out-of-season by reservation.

Brier Island Whale & Seabird Cruises Ltd. ♦ p. 78
Westport, Nova Scotia B0V 1H0
(902) 839-2995
Offering cruises that are professionally guided and narrated by researchers and scientists from the Brier Island Ocean Study, an organization dedicated to research, education, and the conservation of seabirds and the marine ecosystem of the Bay of Fundy. June-Oct. $30. Twice daily.

Broadstreet Cafe ✖ p. 93
Greg and Theresa Saunders
Cornwallis Inn, 325 Main Street
Kentville, Nova Scotia B4N 1K5
(902) 678-9557
Located in the historic Cornwallis Inn, Broadstreet Cafe has earned a reputation for excellent cuisine. The menu expresses the creativity of owner/chef Greg Saunders, offering a balance of fresh seafood, poultry, beef and homemade pastas, all prepared in exciting ways. Sample our fresh desserts and fine wines. Open all week, year-round, 11-9:30. Exit 12 from 101, 2 miles on Route 1.

Carriage House Gallery and Kipawo Arts Centre ■ ♦ p. 101
246 Main Street
Wolfville, Nova Scotia B0P 1X0
(902) 542-3500
Located in Kipawo Arts Centre (along with the Book Shop and Theatre) the Gallery, with branches in Halifax and Lunenburg, is the highlight of this university town with the "smallest natural harbour in the world". It has earned a reputation for original paintings, prints, fabric art and sculpture by Maritime artists. Call for hours or an appointment.

Country Barn Antiques ■ p. 102
Ken Bezanson
135 Main Street
Port Williams, Nova Scotia B0P 1T0
(902) 542-9812
On a landscaped property, this four-storey 1860 post-and-beam barn is impressive in itself. A gallery effect is created with railings and newel posts from old houses and churches. Formal and country furniture in room settings. Glass, silver, brass and china displayed in showcases. Probably the largest such shop in the province. Year-round.

Edgemere Crafts Limited ■ p. 104
Janet Muttart
Starr's Point Road, R.R. #1
Port Williams, Nova Scotia B0P 1T0
(902) 542-5947
In the century-old red barn, adjacent to the Prescott House Museum, Edgemere provides a variety of quality local handcrafts and art – quilts, hand-painted garments, smocking, weaving, hooked rugs, handknits, wood carvings, sculptures, pottery, rough and polished local amethyst and agate, paintings by well-known artists. May 15-Oct 15, 9:30-5. (Sun 1-5) Exit 11 off Hwy 101 to Rte 358.

Edgemere Gallery & Gifts ■ p. 104
Janet Muttart
Town Square, 10 Webster Street
Kentville, Nova Scotia B4N 1H7
(902) 678-9566
A gallery of fine art and handcrafts in Kentville's fashionable new Town Square complex. Features award-winning artists and artisans from Atlantic Canada. Original paintings, prints, terracotta and bronze sculptures, fine porcelain, woven tapestries, quilted images and decorative art, carvings, pewter and fine woollens. Wheelchair access and spacious free parking.

Ewe Wear ■
Katharine Evans p. 92
87 Commercial Street, Box 548
Middleton, Nova Scotia B0S 1P0
(902) 825-4743
Katharine Evans has taken a by-product from the family sheep farms and created "ewe-nique" ideas from cuddly sheepskin, including wonderful teddy bears for all ages. Also sewn on the premises are slippers and mitts, bootees and hats. Each year's wool clip supplies new wool blankets and knitting yarns. Exit 18A from Hwy 101. Year-round. Mon-Sat, 9-5.

The Farmhouse Inn ● ★
Carolyn and Ken Clark, Innkeepers p. 107
1057 Main Street, Box 38
Canning, Nova Scotia B0P 1H0 (902) 582-7900
This restored 200-year-old farmhouse in the historic Annapolis Valley, close to antique and craft shops, historic sites, beaches, parks, cycling and hiking trails, is a popular 'get-away' spot. Down-home country elegance with flowers, books, music and candlelight. Charming rooms with private baths. Family suites available. Full gourmet breakfast, afternoon tea. Special suppers by reservation. Year-round. VISA, M/C. ★★★ (I/B&B)

Firefighters Museum of Nova Scotia ♦
Nova Scotia Museum Complex p. 68
451 Main Street
Yarmouth, Nova Scotia B5A 1G9
(902) 742-5525
Canada's only Provincial Firefighters Museum. Examples of fire engines used in Nova Scotia since 1819, such as a Hopwood and Tilley hand-drawn pumper. Many smaller items on display including photos of many famous fire scenes. Changing national exhibits, a library and gift shop. Open year-round. Admission charge.

Harbourview Inn ▲ ★
Mona and Philip Webb p. 83
Box 39
Smith's Cove, Nova Scotia B0S 1S0
(902) 245-5686
A summer inn since the turn of the century, Harbourview offers 12 guest rooms with private baths, including family suites. Facilities include a licensed dining room, pool, tennis court and tidal beach. Easy access to Upper Clements Park, whale watching, scenic Bear River, historic Annapolis Royal and Digby-Saint John ferry. Exit 24 or 25 off Rte 101. June 1-mid Oct. ★★★ (I/B&B)

The Moorings ●
Susan and Nathaniel Tileston p. 90
Box 118
Granville Ferry, Nova Scotia B0S 1K0
(902) 532-2146
Originally the home of a master mariner, Joseph Hall, this century-old home overlooks the Annapolis Basin and historic Annapolis Royal. Furnished with distinctive antiques and contemporary art, The Moorings offers a full breakfast, fireplace and library. Three rooms, 2 private 1/2 baths, 2 full shared baths. May-Oct. VISA.

Mountain Gap Inn & Resort ▮ ★
Ann Goddard, Managing Director (Innkeeper) p. 84
Box 40
Smith's Cove, Nova Scotia B0S 1S0
(902) 245-5841/1-800-565-5020
Established in 1915, this village-like resort has rooms, cottages and suites. Situated by tidal ocean walking beach with outdoor pool, tennis, children's playground, lawn games. Nearby golf, fishing and boating. Full-service licensed dining room. Packages and meal plans. Recreation and social director. Rates from $67 to $140 (Can). Open mid-May to mid-Oct. ★★★ (R)

The Olde 1890 Village Inn ▲ ★
Bob and Dixie Van p. 76
Sandy Cove
Digby Neck, Nova Scotia B0V 1E0
(902) 834-2202
Celebrating 100 years of hospitality! We offer comfort, character and warmth. "Everything up to date and an excellent table." Licensed dining room, giftshop. The Inn offers 6 rooms; Captain Billy's 7; all private baths, some fireplaces. Honeymoon cottage, Franklin fireplace. Two 2-bedroom cottages. Wicker sunporch. Whale watching,fishing, swimming, biking, hiking, canoeing, tennis. May-Oct. ★★★ (I/B&B)

Pilgrim's Rest Bed & Breakfast ●
Bill and Lynda MacDonald p. 108
Box 177
Canning, Nova Scotia B0P 1H0
(902) 582-3258
This Victorian mansard-roofed house retains its original interior elegance through elaborate cornices, elegant mahogany staircases, marble fireplaces and European antique furnishings. Three double rooms; 2 baths. Full or continental breakfast; evening tea. In-ground pool, large patio. Single $40; double $50. Year-round.

The Pines Resort Hotel ▮ ★
Maurice G. Thiebaut p. 72
Box 70, Shore Road
Digby, Nova Scotia B0V 1A0
(902) 245-2511
A splendid mix of comfortable accommodations, superb cuisine, recreational activities and a commitment to friendly, professional service makes The Pines special. An ideal setting for a family vacation or a romantic get-away. Convention facilities for up to 300. Local attractions include whale watching, deep-sea fishing, historical sites and the Theme Park. Open June-Oct. ★★★★ (R)

The Planters' Barracks ▲ ★
Jennie and Allen Sheito p. 105
Starr's Point Road, R.R. 1
Port Williams, Nova Scotia B0P 1T0
(902) 542-7879
Oldest building in Nova Scotia restored as a country inn (1778). 6 spacious rooms with full private baths. Provincial heritage property furnished with Nova Scotia antiques. Beautiful rural setting overlooking Minas Basin. Traditional country breakfast featuring homemade jams and jellies and seasonal fruit. Tennis, bicycles, BBQ, licensed. Owners bilingual. $49-$75. Major credit cards. Year-round. ★★★★ (I/B&B)

Queen Anne Inn ●
Leslie J. Langille p. 87
494 Upper George Street, Box 218
Annapolis Royal, Nova Scotia B0S 1A0
(902) 532-7850
A restored Victorian mansion in the "Second Empire" style, built circa 1865 as a wedding present to Mr. Norman Richie from his father. The inn features 10 large guest rooms, all with private baths and furnished with period antiques. Convenient location, short walk to Historic Gardens. Open year-round.

Tattingstone Inn ▲ ✖ ★
Betsey Harwood p. 96
434 Main Street, Box 98
Wolfville, Nova Scotia B0P 1X0
(902) 542-7696; Fax 542-4427
Offering luxurious accommodation in the tradition of the English country house. Superb, traditionally prepared cuisine is complimented by an outstanding selection of wines and spirits. Rooms are tastefully decorated with 18th century antiques and works of art, providing every modern comfort. Heated swimming pool, tennis court and steam room. Open year-round. Rates $68-$98. Cottage $125. ★★★★ (I/B&B)

Thistle Down Inn ●
Lisa Hayden **p. 71**
98 Montague Row, Box 508
Digby, Nova Scotia B0V 1A0
(902) 245-4490
Digby's only inn, this period-furnished Edwardian home with panoramic views of the harbour and Annapolis Basin is located on a historical walking tour. Large comfortable rooms with shared baths. Living room with VCR and cable TV. Rates include full breakfast and evening tea with homemade specialties. Croquet, bicycle rentals, whale-watching tours. All major cards. Year-round. Off-season rates.

The Tolmie Gallery at Saratoga ■
Patricia Fisher **p. 91**
RR #3
Bridgetown, Nova Scotia B0S 1C0
(902) 665-4508
The Gallery is situated in a fully restored heritage home that approaches its third century. Set amongst the rolling countryside of the Annapolis Valley near Bridgetown, the property provides the perfect backdrop to the realist art of Ken Tolmie and Ted Colyer. Hwy 201 at Carleton Corner. Open daily April to Dec; Mon-Fri 2-5, Sat-Sun 1-7.

Victoria's Historic Inn ▲●★
Carol and Urbain Cryan **p. 98**
416 Main Street, Box 308
Wolfville, Nova Scotia B0P 1X0
(902) 542-5744
An exceptional Victorian home and registered heritage property, this three-storey landmark and coachhouse offers 15 rooms, many furnished with traditional antiques and all with private baths. The fully licensed dining room offers gourmet dining by candlelight in a refined and relaxed atmosphere. Colour cable TV. Within walking distance of Acadia University. VISA, M/C. Year-round. ★★★ (I/B&B, H/M)

The Weave Shed ■
Denise Aspinall **p. 100**
215 Main Street, Box 893
Wolfville, Nova Scotia B0P 1X0
(902) 542-5504
This six-year-old artisans' co-operative showcases the work of its seven members, as well as other Nova Scotia crafts. Originally emphasizing weaving, the shop has now diversified to include pottery, leatherwork, jewellery and stained glass, along with woven, silk, knitted and sewn garments. Year-round.

Westport Inn B&B and Restaurant ●✖■
Rollie and Nancy Swift **p. 80**
161 Second Street, Box 1226
Westport, Brier Island, Nova Scotia B0V 1H0
(902) 839-2675
Located on Brier Island, this 100-year-old inn is beautifully restored, decorated in country style and furnished with antiques. The inn has 3 bedrooms (one with private bath) plus inviting sitting and TV rooms and sun parlour. Facilities include restaurant, local crafts, gift and grocery items and deck with outdoor dining. $35 single, $45 double, $10 per extra person, includes full breakfast. VISA.

The Wood Studio ■
Ron Gillis and Darlene Winters **p. 70**
Box 280, Route 1
Meteghan, Nova Scotia B0W 2J0
(902) 645-3417
Set in the heart of the Acadian Shore and housed in a century-old restored creamery, this unique country shop carries one-of-a-kind, new and old folk-art, a good selection of antiques and collectibles, new and old quilts and quality handcrafts. Open daily May-Oct. By chance or appointment Nov-April, or at any time.

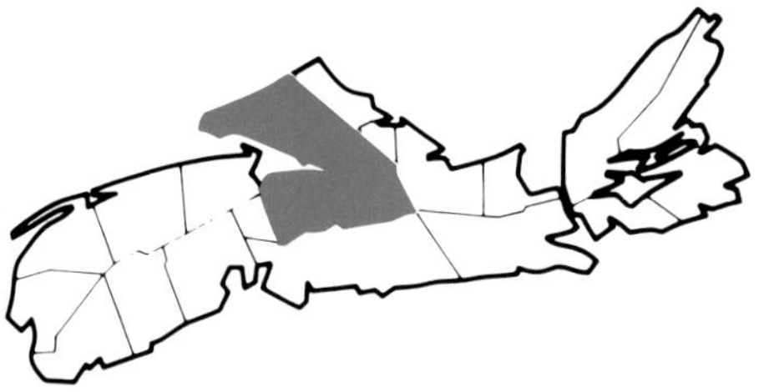

Grade Star Descriptions

★	*Basic, clean, comfortable accommodation*
★★	*Basic, clean, comfortable accommodation with some amenities*
★★★	*Better quality accommodation; greater range of facilities and services*
★★★★	*High quality accommodation; extended range of facilities, amenities and guest services*
★★★★★	*Deluxe accommodation; the greatest range of facilities, amenities and guest services*

- ● Bed & Breakfast
- ▲ Inns
- ♦ Museum/Attraction
- ■ Shop/Gallery
- ✖ Restaurant/Lounge
- ▮ Resort
- ★ Atlantic Canada Accommodations Grading Program

Please Note: All listings appear in alphabetical order.

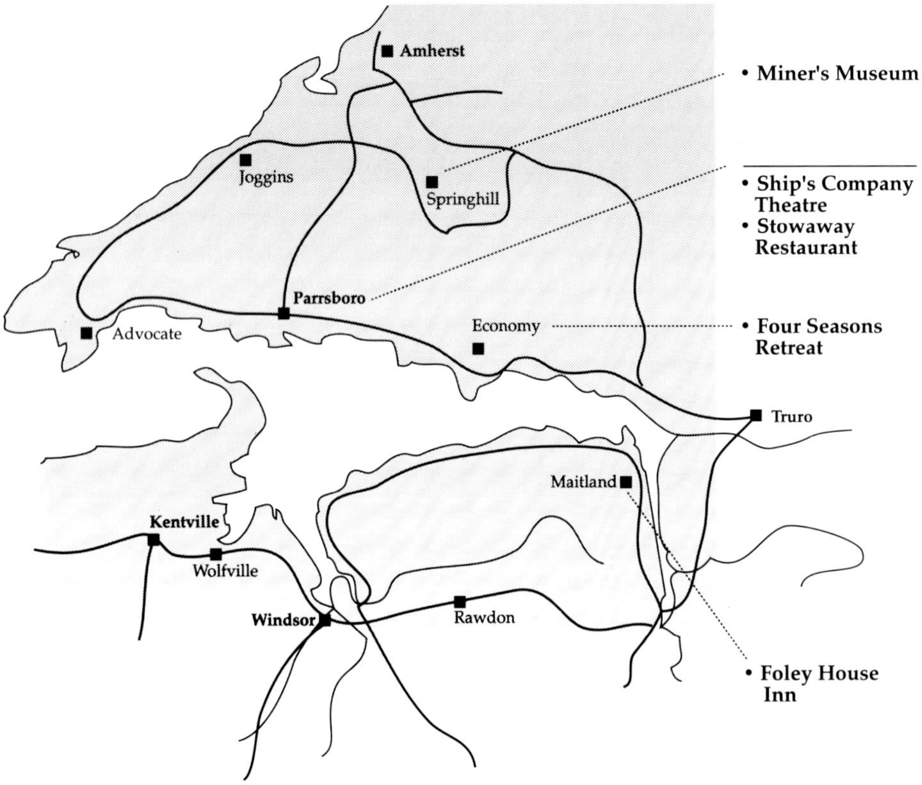

Foley House Inn ▲★
John and Jean Hicks p. 112
Box 58, Maitland, Nova Scotia B0N 1T0
(902) 261-2844 and 261-2302
Walk and view the world's highest tides from this 1830's home in the heart of a shipbuilding community. Lounge with TV. Licensed restaurant open May-Oct 11-9 daily. Private bath: dbl $50; sgl $43. Shared bath: dbl $40; sgl $35. Cot $12. Children under 12 $6. Breakfast incl. Exit 10 and 14 off Hwy 102 to Rtes 236 and 215. Rte 215 from Windsor off Hwy 101. Call for reservations and parties.
★★★ (I/B&B)

Four Seasons Retreat ▲★
Gordon and Maureen Matthews p. 113
Cove Road, RR #1
Economy, Nova Scotia B0M 1J0, (902) 647-2628
Whether you're looking for overnight accommodations or a quiet vacation spot, Four Seasons Retreat is for you. Six fully equipped, two-bedroom cottages, complete with electric heat and airtight stoves, surrounded by woods and facing Cobequid Bay. Ideal for spring fishing, summers on the beach, autumn hunting and hiking, and cross country skiing when the snow flies. Located on Hwy 2. May-March. VISA, M/C, AMX. ★★★ (SL/C)

The Ship's Company Theatre ♦
Michele Inglis (manager) p. 114
38 Main Street, Box 275, Parrsboro, Nova Scotia B0M 1S0 (902) 254-3000 (box office)
Step aboard the M.V. Kipawo and embark on a unique voyage in live theatre. Every July and August, the decks of the historic ferry resound with applause. The Ship's Company Theatre promotes Maritime theatre and talent in an intimate and unusual setting. Show times: Tuesday to Saturday 8 p.m., Saturday and Sunday matinees 2 p.m. Group discounts available. For more information or reservations, please call the box office.

Springhill Miners' Museum ♦
Springhill, Nova Scotia p. 116
(902) 597-3449/2873
Coal mining has been a way of life and a cause of heartache in Springhill for 140 years. Study the exhibits; meet, talk and explore the Syndicate Mine in safety with the experienced miners now working as tour guides at the museum. Swing a pick at the coalface and take home a souvenir lump of Springhill coal. Protective clothing provided. Exhibits, souvenirs, crafts. Adults $3, children $2. 30% discount for bus tours, driver and guide free.

Stowaway Restaurant ✖
Carole and Cathy Henwood p. 115
Lower Main Street
Parrsboro, Nova Scotia B0M 1S0
(902) 254-3371
Seafood and home-baked breads and desserts are house specialties in this licensed dining room with its panoramic view of the Minas Basis. You can also buy baked goods to take with you on your trip. Just minutes from the Ship's Company Theatre. Wheelchair accessible. Bus tours welcome. Open year-round: June 1-Sept 30, 9 a.m.-11 p.m.; Oct 1 - May 31, 9 a.m.-8 p.m. VISA, M/C, AMX.

Sunrise Trail

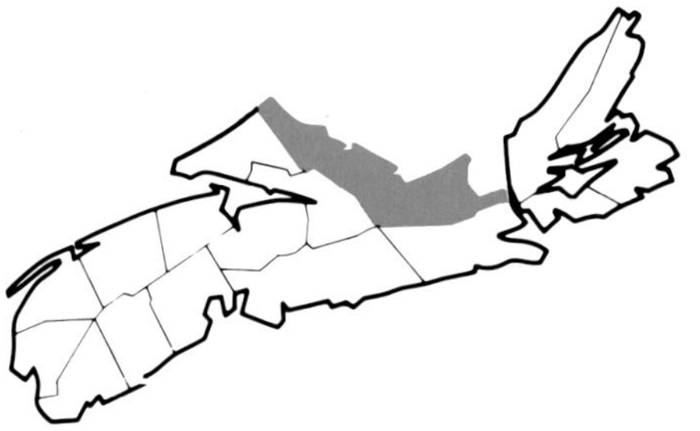

Grade Star Descriptions

★	*Basic, clean, comfortable accommodation*
★★	*Basic, clean, comfortable accommodation with some amenities*
★★★	*Better quality accommodation; greater range of facilities and services*
★★★★	*High quality accommodation; extended range of facilities, amenities and guest services*
★★★★★	*Deluxe accommodation; the greatest range of facilities, amenities and guest services*

- ● Bed & Breakfast
- ▲ Inns
- ♦ Museum/Attraction
- ■ Shop/Gallery
- ✖ Restaurant/Lounge
- ▮ Resort
- ★ Atlantic Canada Accommodations Grading Program

Please Note: All listings appear in alphabetical order.

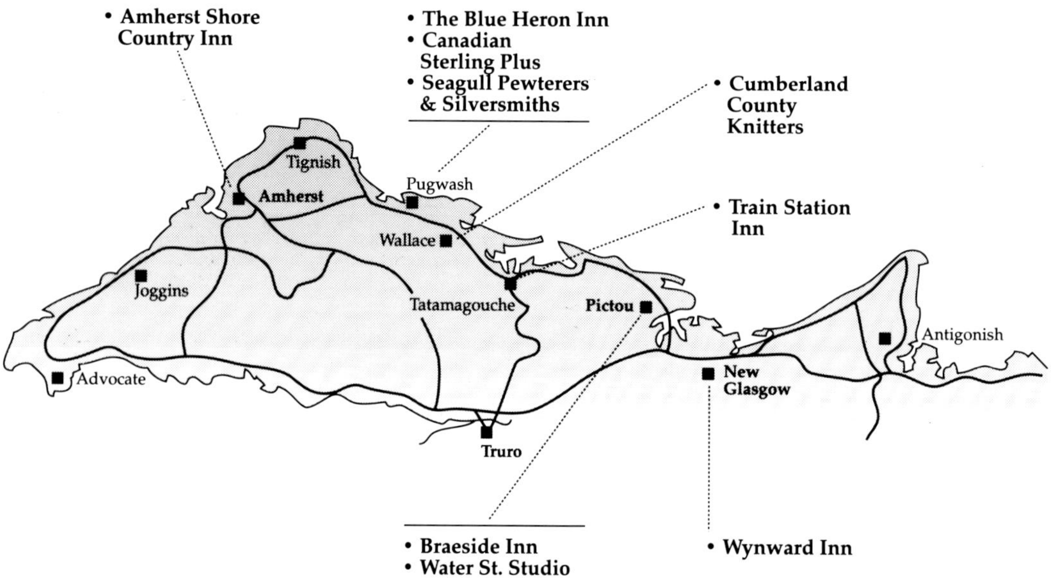

Amherst Shore Country Inn ▲★
Donna Laceby **p. 120**
R.R. 2
Amherst, Nova Scotia B4H 3X9
(902) 667-4800
A charming country inn with a renowned gourmet dining room featuring a panoramic view of the Northumberland Strait. Relax in one of the inn's uniquely furnished rooms or seaside cottage. Each evening at 7:30 the inn serves a four-course dinner by reservation only. 20 minutes from Amherst or Pugwash. Hwy 366 at Lorneville. Seasonal.
★★★★ (I/B&B)

The Blue Heron Inn ●
Bonnie Bond and John Caraberis **p. 123**
Box 405
Pugwash, Nova Scotia B0K 1L0
(902) 243-2900 or 243-2516 (off-season)
This century-old restored inn features five tastefully decorated rooms, continental breakfast included. In the village of Pugwash, it is close to beaches, golf, tennis and several craft shops. June 1-Labour Day.

Canadian Sterling Plus ■
Peter Finley **p. 121**
Durham Street, Box 148
Pugwash, Nova Scotia B0K 1L0
(902) 243-2563
A manufacturing outlet of precious metal jewellery. Visitors are invited to stop by this unique shop to watch jewellery being hand-made on the premises. Jewellery manufactured in gold, silver, crystals and precious stones. Earrings, rings, pins, thimbles and more. Located just off Route 6 in downtown Pugwash. Open year-round. VISA, M/C.

Cumberland County Knitters ■
Richard and Pat Ratcliffe **p. 124**
Box 246
Wallace, Nova Scotia B0K 1Y0
(902) 257-2819
This classic line of Fairisle knitwear, 100% virgin wool, is fashioned in tones of the Atlantic seashore by experienced knitters. Sweaters, matching headwear, mitts, scarves, socks, legwarmers. Men, women, children. Sunrise Trail 40 miles east of Amherst, about 40 miles west of Pictou. Year-round. Winter months by "opportunity".

Pictou Town Braeside Inn ▲★
Artists Tom MacKay and Claude Ferland **p. 126**
80 Front Street, Box 1810
Pictou, Nova Scotia B0K 1H0 (902) 485-5046
Formerly l'Auberge, this comfortably refurbished inn stands on a 4-acre hillside, overlooking Pictou Harbour. 20 guest rooms with private bath, formal 100-seat dining room and lounge. 50-seat greenhouse dining room. $55-$80. 5 minutes from PEI ferry terminal. Instruction in oils, acrylics and drawing available. May-Dec. Off-season rates from Oct 15.
★★★ (I/B&B)

Seagull Pewterers and Silversmiths ■
John Caraberis and Bonnie Bond **p. 122**
Box 370
Pugwash, Nova Scotia B0K 1L0
(902) 243-2516
This tasteful gift shop offers a blend of fine crafts and antiques, including pewter wares and silver jewellery pieces made on the premises. Pewter includes picture frames and a range of holloware. Located on Route 6, west of the bridge, on Pugwash Harbour. Open daily.

Train Station Inn ●★
James and Shelley LeFresne **p. 125**
27 Station Rd., Box 67, Tatamagouche
Nova Scotia B0K 1V0
(902) 657-3222
This century-old train station has been restored and furnished with antiques that capture the elegance of the station. The Inn's three bedrooms have private baths. Evening tea is served in the parlour. Enjoy your breakfast in the elegance of the dining room or in the sun on the balcony. Year-round.
★★★★ (I/B&B).

Water Street Studio ■
115 Water Street, Box 1442 **p. 130**
Pictou, Nova Scotia B0K 1H0
(902) 485-8398
This Scottish stone house was built in 1825 as a storefront and residence. Owned by railway pioneer, Lord Strathcona, and used as a sheriff's office and bank. Now a co-operative craft shop featuring handmade clothes, weaving, pottery, watercolours, jewellery and other local artworks. Year-round.

Wynward Inn ●
Dorothy Leahy-Walsh **p. 128**
71 Stellarton Road
New Glasgow, Nova Scotia B2H 1L7
(902) 752-4527
In the heart of New Glasgow, the Inn has been welcoming visitors since 1930. Each room in the circa 1880 house is individually decorated with four-posters in many bedrooms. The homey atmosphere includes barbecue, picnic tables, swings and a swimming pool. Reasonable rates include a light breakfast. Year-round. Exit 23 or 24 from 104: Exit 2 from 106.

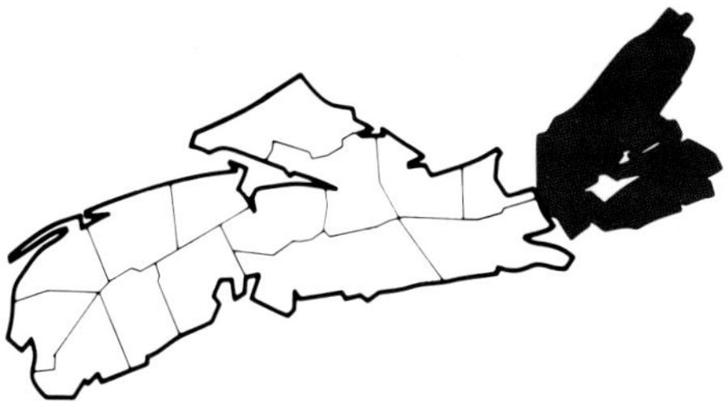

Grade Star Descriptions

★	*Basic, clean, comfortable accommodation*
★★	*Basic, clean, comfortable accommodation with some amenities*
★★★	*Better quality accommodation; greater range of facilities and services*
★★★★	*High quality accommodation; extended range of facilities, amenities and guest services*
★★★★★	*Deluxe accommodation; the greatest range of facilities, amenities and guest services*

- ● Bed & Breakfast
- ▲ Inns
- ♦ Museum/Attraction
- ■ Shop/Gallery
- ✖ Restaurant/Lounge
- ▮ Resort
- ★ Atlantic Canada Accommodations Grading Program

Please Note: All listings appear in alphabetical order.

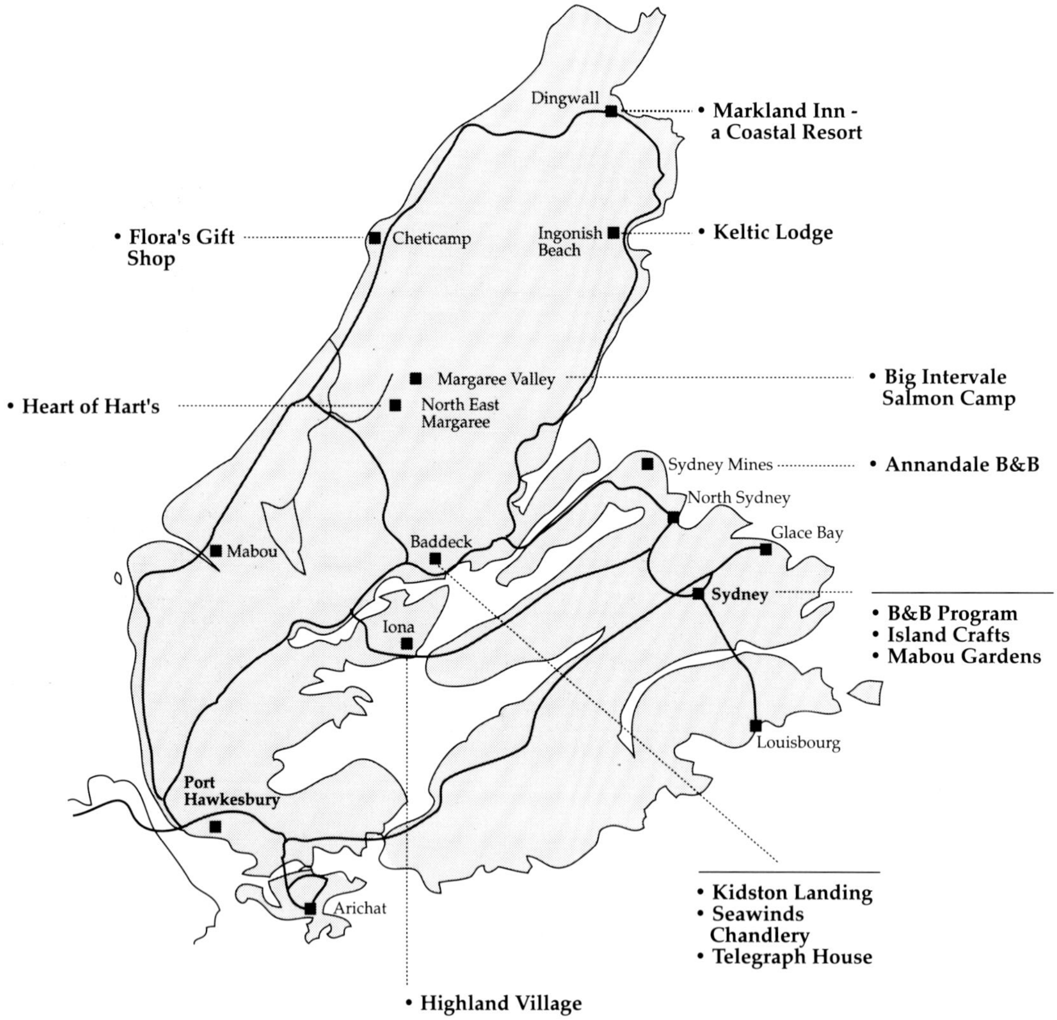

Annandale Bed & Breakfast ●
Scott Phillips and Meg Sargent p. 148
157 Shore Road
Sydney Mines, Nova Scotia B1V 1A9
(902) 544-1052
This antique-filled 1879 Queen Anne home – situated in Sydney Mines, 3km from the Newfoundland ferry terminal – commands a panoramic view of Sydney Harbour and the sea beyond. Warm hospitality and comfortably appointed rooms with shared bath. Central to all major Cape Breton attractions. Rates include full breakfast. Year-round.

Big Intervale Salmon Camps Inc. ▲ ✖
Bill Davidson p. 136
West Big Intervale Road, RR#1
Margaree Valley, Nova Scotia B0E 2C0
(902) 248-2275
Located on 60 wooded acres nestled between two mountains, Big Intervale Salmon Camp provides fine food and quality accommodation on the banks of the beautiful Margaree River. Atlantic salmon angling, bird watching, hiking or just relaxing in the great outdoors. Near beaches and historic sites. Dining room and lounge are fully licensed.

Cape Breton Bed & Breakfast Program ● ▲
Enterprise Cape Breton Corporation p. 150
Box 1750
Sydney, Nova Scotia B1P 6T7
1-800-565-9460
Canada's first Bed & Breakfast was established in Cape Breton's Northern Highlands about 18 years ago, beginning a tradition of down-home hospitality and comfort that is enriched every year. Today there are over 65 Cape Breton homes in the program, each providing comfortable accommodations at reasonable rates, with special touches of Island charm.

Flora's Gift Shop ■
Rene LeFort p. 137
Main Street, Box 316
Cheticamp, Nova Scotia B0E 1H0
(902) 224-3139
Largest selection of Cheticamp hooked rugs, ranging in size from coasters to rugs. Demonstrations of this famous Acadian art using hand-dyed burlap. Other local crafts and souvenirs. 3000 square feet of shopping space, ample parking. Bus tours welcome. Ice cream parlour and refreshments. Point Cross, 2 miles south of Cheticamp on the Cabot Trail. April-Oct: 8-8; Nov-March: by appointment.

Heart of Hart's Tourist Home ● ★
Laird and Mary Hart p. 135
North East Margaree, Nova Scotia B0E 2H0
(902) 248-2765
The easiest way to find us is by travelling the Trans Canada Highway, Route 105 to Junction 7 of Nyanza. Turn north on the Cabot Trail, 19 miles, turn right at our sign and go 1/4 mile to Heart of Hart's. Full country breakfast is served each day and is included in the rate for the room. May 15-Nov 15.
★★★ (I/B&B)

Island Crafts Ltd. ■
Dorothy Phillips (manager/owner) p. 149
329 Charlotte Street
Sydney, Nova Scotia B1P 1E1
(902) 539-4424
This craft shop in downtown Sydney offers a wide array of crafts from Cape Breton Island and the rest of the Maritimes. Handknit sweaters, from fisherman knits to mohair. Cheticamp hooking, Island literature, a wide range of pottery, quilts etc. Savour the flavour! Mon-Sat. Year-round.

Keltic Lodge ▮
Alexander MacClure p. 140
Box 70
Ingonish Beach, Nova Scotia B0C 1L0
(902) 285-2880
Some of the most spectacular country in eastern Canada is the setting for this fine old lodge and its modern companion, the White Birch Inn, which adds another 40 air-conditioned rooms. Tennis, golf and nature walks are at hand, along with cross country trails and Cape Smokey skiing for winter enjoyment. Exquisite dining. June-Oct; Jan-March.
★★★★ (R)

Kidston Landing Country Store ■
Peggy and Bruce Anderson p. 142
Chebucto Street, Box 100
Baddeck, Nova Scotia B0E 1B0
(902) 295-2868
Here you'll find a country flavour in the centre of town. A delightful choice of clothing and gifts that features woollens, small pine pieces and a range of Atlantic Canada crafts – as well as other good Canadian giftwares. Open year-round.

Mabou Gardens ■ ♦
Florence Sauler p. 134
R.R. 4, Site 18, Box A, Comp. 0
Sydney, Nova Scotia B1P 6G6
(902) 562-6000
Spend a leisurely time looking at our large array of Nova Scotia and Maritime crafts. We have silk flower arrangements, also fresh flowers for all occasions. Our quilts are especially nice and priced to please. Gypsum figurines, quilted place mats, etc., plush toys, pottery and much more. The Garden Centre is stocked with plants, soil and everything a gardener could want. Open year-round.

The Markland - a Coastal Resort ▮ ✖
Ann MacLean (manager) p. 138
Dingwall, Nova Scotia B0C 1G0
(902) 383-2246
Welcome to Aspy Valley where the mountains touch the sea! Walk along the miles of crescent beach, relax in a luxury log suite or housekeeping cottage, hike on 70 acres of woodland property, go for a row or try your hand at fishing on the Middle Aspy River. Major attractions – Cape Breton Highlands National Park, whale watching, local history museum. Just a few miles from Cape North.

Nova Scotia Highland Village ♦
Brian McCormack (Manager) p. 146
R.R. 2, Rte. 223
Iona, Nova Scotia B0A 1L0
(902) 725- 2272
This museum highlights the area's rich Scottish history and culture. The Village contains nine historic buildings including the only known reconstructed 'Black House' in North America and a working period forge. In our reception centre you'll find displays, a gift counter and computer-assisted genealogical information. You'll meet friendly staff along the way. Open June 15-Sept 15. Mon-Sat 9-5, Sun 11-6.

Seawinds Chandlery ■
Bruce and Peggy Anderson p. 143
Government Wharf, Box 100
Baddeck, Nova Scotia B0E 1B0
(902) 295-2205
Enjoy shopping in this vintage wharf warehouse – your bonus is a superb view across the water from the Chandlery doors. A wide choice of clothing and giftware with a nautical flavour, including rainwear and oiled sweaters. June 1- Oct 15.

Telegraph House ▲ ★
Buddy and Mary Dunlop p. 144
Chebucto Street, Box 8
Baddeck, Nova Scotia B0E 1B0
(902) 295-9988
In the heart of Baddeck, a quaint Victorian house where Dr. Alexander Graham Bell chose to stay, royalty chose to dine and where celebrities choose to be wed. 130 years of gracious hospitality. One of the finest authentically historic dining rooms on the East Coast, offering a truly homemade Maritime menu. Near beaches, parks, tennis, golf, trails. VISA, M/C. Year-round. ★★★ (H/M, I/B&B).

Marine Drive

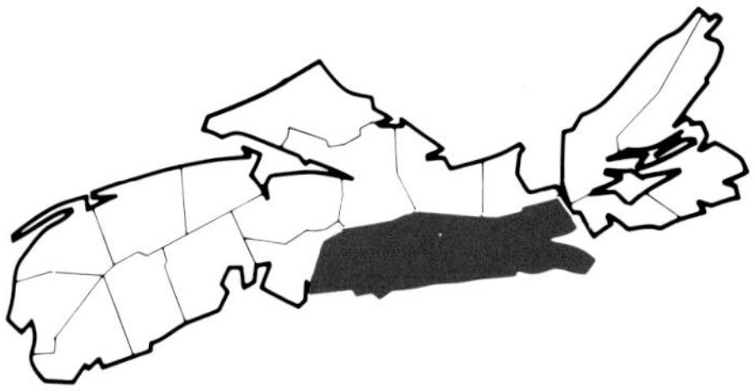

Grade Star Descriptions

★	*Basic, clean, comfortable accommodation*
★★	*Basic, clean, comfortable accommodation with some amenities*
★★★	*Better quality accommodation; greater range of facilities and services*
★★★★	*High quality accommodation; extended range of facilities, amenities and guest services*
★★★★★	*Deluxe accommodation; the greatest range of facilities, amenities and guest services*

- ● Bed & Breakfast
- ▲ Inns
- ♦ Museum/Attraction
- ■ Shop/Gallery
- ✖ Restaurant/Lounge
- ▮ Resort
- ★ Atlantic Canada Accommodations Grading Program

Please Note: All listings appear in alphabetical order.

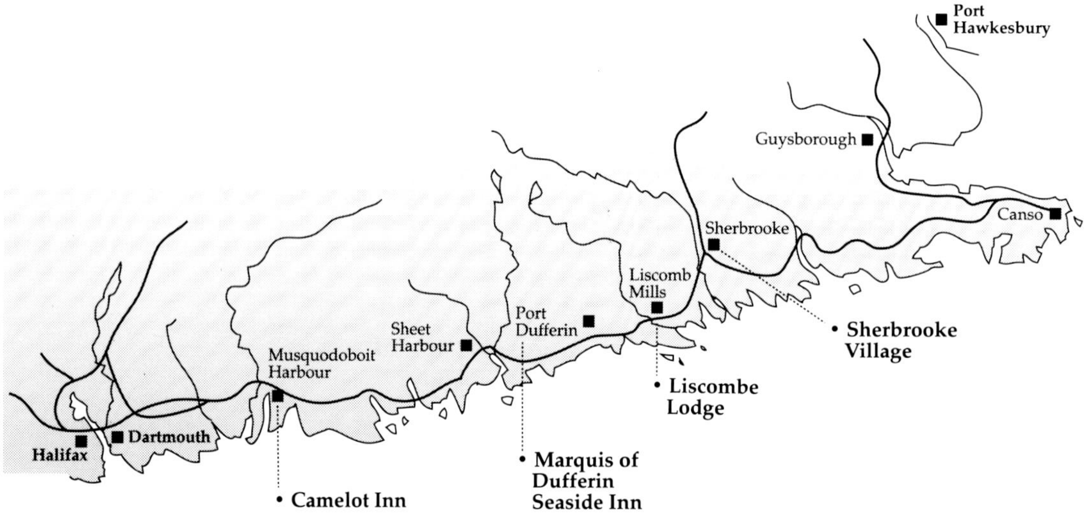

Camelot Inn ▲★
Charlie Holgate p. 154
Box 31
Musquodoboit Harbour, Nova Scotia B0J 2L0
(902) 889-2198
This gracious house is tucked in a secluded bend of the Musquodoboit River. Five rooms with three shared bathrooms. Comfortable lounge with fireplace and extensive library. Hearty breakfast, superb candlelit dinners in licensed dining room. Good birdwatching. 7 1/2 miles from Martinique Beach. Dinner by appointment only. VISA, M/C. Year-round.
★★★ (I/B&B)

Liscombe Lodge ▮★
David M. Evans p. 158
Hwy 7, Liscomb Mills, Nova Scotia B0J 2A0
(902) 779-2307; Fax 779-2700
Tucked away in the clear, wooded seclusion of the Eastern Shore, Liscombe Lodge is the ultimate outdoor family retreat. A haven for hikers, canoeists and all lovers of the outdoors. Boat rentals and marina mooring facilities. Children's playground, tennis court. Superb dining complements country atmosphere. Choose accommodations in the lodge, cottages or chalets, overlooking scenic river. All major cards. June-Oct. ★★★ (R)

Marquis of Dufferin Seaside Inn ▲★
Michael and Eve Concannon p. 156
Hwy 7, R.R. 1
Port Dufferin, Nova Scotia B0J 2R0
(902) 654-2696
Dine in our heritage residence listed in *Where to Eat in Canada*. Relax with an aperitif on the enclosed verandah. 14 comfortable units, 8 with private balconies and superb ocean view. Breakfast included in 8-unit room rates. Lawn games, hiking, fishing, birding, sailing. TIANS Innkeeper Award 1988. 85 miles east of Halifax and airport. Late May to mid-Oct. VISA, M/C. ★★★ H/M)

Sherbrooke Village ♦
Nova Scotia Museum Complex p. 160
Route 7, Box 295
Sherbrooke, N.S. B0J 3C0
(902) 522-2400
A picturesque lumbering and shipbuilding village restored to the late 19th century when goldmining briefly transformed it into a boom town. Over 20 buildings on their original sites and open to the public; some are wheelchair accessible. After your tour, enjoy refreshments in the *What Cheer* tearoom and visit the Emporium for crafts. Bus tours welcome with reservations. May 15-Oct 15, 9:30-5:30 daily.

Country Inns, Bed & Breakfast and much more

Country Inns, Bed & Breakfast and much more

All book photographs by Sherman Hines available from:

Masterfile, Stock Photo Library
15 Yonge Street, Suite 200
Toronto, Canada
M5B 2E7

Information on all other photographs may be obtained by writing directly to the publisher.

James-StoneHouse Publications Ltd.
PO Box 428
Dartmouth, Nova Scotia
Canada B2Y 3Y5

Legend

Bkg: *Background*
In: *Inset*
InT: *Inset Top*
InM: *Inset Middle*
InB: *Inset Bottom*
T: *Top*
B: *Bottom*
Lt: *Left*
Rt: *Right*

Sherman Hines: Cover, 4-5, 6-7, 8-9, 10-11, 12, 13B, 18-19, 21InTInBBkg, 30Bkg, 31, 35, 36Bkg, 37InBRt, 66-67, 69, 72-75, 82B, 87Bkg, 94-95, 109, 110-111, 117, 118-119, 120, 122, 123T, 126-127, 131, 132-133, 152-153, 154-155, 182

Michael Concannon: 156-157Bkg, 156InB, 157InT

Education Media Services, Province of Nova Scotia: 42

Blaine Fisher: 16Bkg, 17BkgIn, 25, 26, 27, 28, 29, 40, 43, 93, 100, 102-103, 104, 105, 106, 107

Owen Fitzgerald: 148

Warren Gordon: 128-129, 131, 132, 136, 137, 138-139, 140InB, 142, 143, 144-145, 146-147, 149, 150, 151

Ben Guinn: 83InT

Carl Haycock: 78-79

Wally Hayes: 140-141Bkg, 141In, 158-159Bkg

Richard Hines: 30In, 32-33, 53In, 54, 55InT, 59

Leo MacDonald: 84InT, 87In

Norman Monroe: 125

Alex Murchison: Title Page, 14In, 15InT, 20Bkg, 23, 24, 34, 36InTInBLtBRt 37BkgInBLt, 38-39, 41, 46-47, 48, 50, 51, 52, 53Bkg, 55Bkg, 56, 71, 76-77, 80-81, 82T, 84-85Bkg, 84InM, 86In, 88-89, 92, 96-97, 98-99, 101, 108, 112, 113, 114, 115, 116, 121, 123B 130, 156InT, 157InB, 160-161

Richard Nicolle: 58, 59, 62-63, 64-65, 68

Nat Tileston: Back Cover, 49, 70, 83BkgInB, 84InB, 85In, 86Bkg, 90, 91

Dale Wilson: 124

Pg.2-3 and 61: **Courtesy of White Point Beach Lodge**

Pg.14-15Bkg, 15InB: **Courtesy of Parks Canada**

Pg.44-45: **Courtesy of The Mainstay Country Inn/Homeport Motel**

Pg. 49: **Courtesy of Snug Harbour Bed & Breakfast**

Pg. 57: **Courtesy of Country Pine Workshop, Giftshop**

Pg. 140InT: **Courtesy of Nova Scotia Department of Tourism & Culture**

Pg. 157InT: **Courtesy of Marquis of Dufferin Seaside Inn**